Right Concentration

Right CONCENTRATION

A Practical Guide to the Jhānas

Leigh Brasington

SHAMBHALA
Boulder
2015

Shambhala Publications, Inc.
4720 Walnut Street
Boulder, Colorado 80301
www.shambhala.com

9 8 7 6 5 4 3 2

Printed in the United States of America

♾ This edition is printed on acid-free paper that meets the American National Standards Institute Z39.48 Standard.
♻ This book is printed on 30% postconsumer recycled paper.
For more information please visit www.shambhala.com.

Distributed in the United States by Penguin Random House LLC
and in Canada by Random House of Canada Ltd

Designed by Greta D. Sibley

Library of Congress Cataloging-in-Publication Data

Brasington, Leigh, author.
Right concentration: a practical guide to the jhanas / Leigh Brasington.
—First edition.
pages cm
Includes bibliographical references and index.
ISBN 978-1-61180-269-6 (paperback: alk. paper)
1. Meditation—Theravada Buddhism. I. Title.
BQ7280.B73 2015
294.3′4435—dc23
2014049333

For my (so-called) students,
in deep appreciation for all they have taught me

Contents

PART TWO

Demystified Jhānas

Abbreviations Used in Textual References

AN	Anguttara-Nikāya (book.verse)
Dhp	*Dhammapada* (verse)
Dhs	*Dhammasaṅgaṇī*
D	Dīgha Nikāya (PTS page references)
DN	Dīgha Nikāya (sutta.verse or sutta.subsection.verse.item)
Iti	Itivuttaka (verse)
MN	Majjhima Nikāya (sutta.verse)
PED	*Pali-English Dictionary* from the Pali Text Society
SN	Saṃyutta Nikāya (sutta.verse)
Snp	Sutta-nipāta (book.sutta)
Ud	Udāna (book.sutta)
Vsm	*Visuddhimagga* (*The Path of Purification* by Buddhaghosa, translated by the Ven. Ñāṇamoli, BPS 1956, 2010)

Preface

NAMO TASSA BHAGAVATO ARAHATO SAMMASAMBUDDHASSA.
Homage to the Blessed One, the Arahat, the Perfectly Awakened Buddha.

THE JHĀNAS are eight altered states of consciousness, brought on via concentration, and each yielding a deeper state of concentration than the previous. In teaching the eightfold path, the Buddha defined right concentration to be the jhānas. The jhānas themselves are not awakening, but they are a skillful means for concentrating the mind in a way that leads in that direction, and they are attainable not only by monastics, but also by many serious lay practitioners.

This book is an attempt to transmit what I have learned about the jhānas into a readable form. Since the jhānas don't lend themselves to "book learning," this attempt is bound to be less than ideal. Nonetheless, I hope to provide at least some useful information about the jhānas and how they can be used on the spiritual path.

This book assumes some familiarity with both meditation and basic Buddhist teachings.* The jhānas are definitely an advanced topic. In gen-

*For an excellent introduction to basic Buddhist teachings, please see the book *Being Nobody, Going Nowhere* by Ayya Khema (Wisdom Publications, 1988).

eral, learning the jhānas comes much more easily for those who have attended at least two one-week or longer silent meditation retreats and have a good daily meditation practice of at least forty-five minutes, preferably longer. So I've written this book for people who have the requisite background for beginning to learn the jhānas. However, if you are primarily interested in learning about the jhānas rather than learning them as a practice, this book should also serve you well.

I have used a number of Pali words, so there is a glossary at the back of this book. It turns out to be easier to be precise by using the words from the suttas than an English word that doesn't really capture the essence of what the Buddha was teaching. The following table should be helpful:

sutta	discourse, teaching
mettā	loving-kindness, unconditional love
samādhi	indistractability, concentration, pulling/gathering together
vitakka	thinking
vicāra	examining
pīti	glee, rapture
sukha	happiness/joy
dukkha	bummer,* unsatisfactoriness, stress, suffering, distress

That last word, *dukkha,* is extremely important. The Buddha said on several occasions that he taught "dukkha and especially the end of dukkha."[1] This book will hopefully show how jhāna practice is very helpful in the quest to gain the deep insights necessary for ending dukkha.

The translations in this book are based on the works of Bhikkhu Bodhi, Maurice Walshe, and Thanissaro Bhikkhu. I have at times altered

* See the essay "*Dukkha* Is a Bummer" at http://leighb.com/bummer.htm for a detailed exploration of why "bummer" is a good translation of *dukkha.*

these translations, occasionally to make something clearer and often to remove the gender specific *he/his,* for which I have substituted *one/one's*—the Pali is simply third person singular and literally could be *he, she,* or *one.* Since this book is written for a general audience, not a male monastic one, and given the centuries of misogynist patriarchy in Buddhism, I am unwilling to write in a way that gives any credence to that particular misunderstanding of the Buddha's teachings. I have also used *they* and *their* as singular gender-neutral pronouns when necessary in order to avoid silliness like *s/he* or *he/she.*

This book is based on the jhāna teachings found in the suttas of the Pali canon. Although at times I use phrases like "the Buddha says" and "the Buddha taught," from a strict scholastic viewpoint, I should be saying something like "suttas say the Buddha says" and "suttas say the Buddha taught." But that seems overly pedantic; I trust you will know that when I say "the Buddha says," I'm just indicating what the suttas record the Buddha as saying.

The jhānas are a controversial topic, and I would not be surprised if what I have written here adds to the controversy. This is not my intent; I only want to share what I have learned so that these wonderfully powerful states can be used successfully by more people on their path toward awakening. One of the most important things to bring on the spiritual path is an open mind. If you are not fully awake right now, you are going to have to change your mind to get there. It is very helpful to remember the line of teaching on views given in the closing verse of the Mettā Sutta (Snp 1.8):

> But when one lives quite free from any view,
> is virtuous, with perfect insight won,
> and greed for sensual desires expelled—
> one surely comes no more to any womb.[2]

May what follows be useful to you on your spiritual journey.

You can find all the web links mentioned in this book at http://rc.leighb.com/links.htm. Bookmark this site and you won't have to type any long, complex web addresses.

—Leigh Brasington

Right Concentration

Introduction

June 4, 1988: It's forty minutes into the forty-five-minute sitting before lunch—and my back is killing me. I slide forward on the little cushion I'm using as a zafu and my sit bones slip onto the mat, but my tailbone remains on the cushion. The result is instantaneous. My hips are thrust forward, correctly aligning my vertebrae and thus relaxing all the muscle tension in my back, and a huge flood of joyous energy fills my whole being. Immediately two thoughts arise: "I'm gonna always sit like this!" and "This must be what that Dutch woman was talking about when she asked that question 'What do I do with all this joy I'm getting?'"

I was at Ajahn Buddhadasa's Wat Suan Mokkh* in southern Thailand, and they told me there that what I was experiencing was called *pīti.* I didn't really understand what was happening—I just knew I liked it and that my motivation for sitting in meditation had changed from doing it because I knew it was good for me, to meditating because I wanted to. I continued to access the pīti once or twice a day for the rest of my stay

* Suan Mokkhabalarama (The Grove of the Power of Liberation), about six kilometers southwest of the village of Chaiya in southern Thailand. It was founded in 1932 by Ajahn Buddhadasa, and when I visited in 1988, it was to attend the ten-day retreat offered to foreigners each month.

at Suan Mokkh, but my access dropped away when my daily meditation practice became more irregular as I continued my Asian travels that year.

Over the course of the next two years, I found I had fairly regular access to the pīti depending on how regular my sitting practice was. I mentioned it to teachers with whom I had interviews on subsequent retreats, but no one really seemed able to give me any advice about what to do next. I remember saying, "It's like I've found the door to the magic castle. I go into the first room and wander around for about ten minutes and then find myself back outside again. I know there's got to be more rooms!"

In May of 1990, I attended a ten-day retreat with Venerable Ayya Khema, who had led the very first retreat I ever attended back in 1985. I remembered she had been a very excellent teacher on that first retreat. So when a friend thrust a flyer into my hands for the 1990 retreat with her, I signed up. I went to my first interview with her, and, after exchanging pleasant courtesies, she said, "Well now, tell me about your meditation."

"I can get to pīti," I replied.

"Good. That's the first jhāna; here's how you do the second." Somebody knew what was happening and furthermore knew what came next! By the end of that retreat, I had access to not only the first and second jhānas, but also the third, fourth, and fifth. And I knew I'd found my teacher.

A year later I sat with Ayya for five weeks. I learned jhānas six, seven, and eight and was thoroughly enjoying running 'em up (one to eight) and running 'em back down (eight to one). Not too long after I gained some skill at doing this, I was again in an interview with Ayya, and she said, "Now you must do insight practice in the same sitting after you do the jhānas."

"But it takes me the whole sitting to go up and back down," I protested.

"Do them faster."

Now, Ayya Khema was not someone you wanted to argue with, so I nodded, said, "Yes, ma'am," and went back to meditating and "doing them faster." That indeed left time for insight practice. And wow! The flood of insights was mind-blowing. The quantity and quality was unlike anything I'd ever experienced before. My fascination with altered states was gone and replaced with a drive to see what I could learn next. By the end of that retreat, I felt for the first time that I had some idea of the basics of what the Buddha taught. I could hang all those lists that had been abstractly floating around, on the pegs of *sīla, samādhi,* and *paññā:* ethical behavior, concentration, and wisdom. But even more important: the insights were life changing; when I got home, my friends could see a difference. My dedication to following the path the Buddha had laid out was now unshakable—and I knew how to proceed.

The Jhānas. Perhaps no aspect of the Buddha's teaching has been both more misunderstood and neglected than right concentration. Yet right concentration is obviously an integral part of the Buddha's path to awakening:* right concentration is the eighth item of the noble† eightfold path and is often exemplified by and even defined as the four jhānas.[1] Before his awakening, after rejecting both the path of sensual indulgence and the path of austerities, the Buddha remembered an incident from his childhood when he had experienced the first jhāna; upon further reflection he concluded, "That is indeed the path to awakening."[2]

---

* Throughout this book, I will use *awakening* rather than the perhaps more familiar *enlightenment* since *enlightenment* is not an accurate translation, having been chosen by the early translators to suggest a connection with the European Enlightenment.

† Although the word *noble* is a correct literal translation, it doesn't really capture all of what is meant. *Ennobling* would be far more elucidating, since practicing in accord with this path will ennoble you. But I will continue to use the more familiar *noble.*

This book is an attempt to rectify the misunderstandings and neglect of the role of concentration in the Buddha's teachings. Part One will provide a practical guide to the jhānas using the material found in the suttas of the Pali canon, supplemented with my practice of these states and my teaching them to over a thousand students during the course of over a hundred meditation retreats. Since the material presented in Part One will be different in some ways from what is traditionally presented when the jhānas are (occasionally) taught, Part Two will take a much closer, in-depth look at the jhānas as presented in the suttas to tease out exactly what is being said there.

The word *jhāna* literally means "meditation."* It comes from the verb *jhāyati,* which means "to meditate." Many times the Buddha would give a dhamma talk and close it by saying, "There are these roots of trees, these empty huts, go meditate (*jhāyati*)."[3] From this usage of *jhāyati,* it seems certain that what the Buddha meant by meditation was jhāna practice.

In the suttas, there are four jhānas and four immaterial states. These eight states are at times presented as a sequence of eight progressively deeper concentration experiences, each one building on the concentration generated by the previous experience. More often they are presented as the four jhānas without any mention of the four immaterial states, and at other times the four immaterial states are presented without any mention of the four jhānas. In modern times (and even as early as the Abhidhamma composition period) these eight states are simply called the *eight jhānas.*

As I discovered back in 1991, the Buddha's teachings can be divided

*From the PTS *Pali-English Dictionary* under *jhāna*: "Literally meditation. But it never means vaguely meditation. It is the technical term for a special religious experience, reached in a certain order of mental states."

into three parts: sīla, samādhi, and pañña: ethical conduct, concentration, and wisdom. Or to put it into the vernacular: clean up your act, concentrate your mind, and use your concentrated mind to investigate reality. The practices the Buddha taught fit neatly into one of the three categories. The precepts* and the brahma-vihāra practices of loving-kindness, compassion, appreciative joy, and equanimity are ethical practices. The brahma-vihāra practices, especially loving-kindness (mettā) practice, can also generate concentration, as do mantra and visualization practices. But most everything else you think of when you hear the word *meditation* are wisdom practices—practices that are intended to help you "see the way things are" (or perhaps more accurately "what's actually happening"). But the Buddha makes it abundantly clear[4] that your examination of reality should be done with a concentrated mind. And the jhānas are the method he taught over and over again for concentrating the mind.

The Pali word *samādhi* is usually translated as "concentration," and that's not a bad translation. But "concentration" has a furrowed-brow connotation. Perhaps a better translation would be "indistractability," which unfortunately is not really an English word. What the Buddha is pointing to with the word *samādhi* is the ability of your mind to not become distracted—the ability of your mind to remain aware of a specific, chosen topic without unintentionally wandering off to some other topic. Although I will use the word "concentration" as a translation of *samādhi* throughout this book, you should strive to keep in mind that it really is referring to a state of indistractability.

Concentration is called both a power and a faculty. In both cases it is defined as the four jhānas,[5] just like right concentration is also defined

---

* See chapter 1, "The Preliminaries," and the web page on the precepts at http://rc.leighb.com/more/The_Precepts.htm for more detailed information.

as the four jhānas.[6] The jhānas are eight altered states of consciousness, brought on via concentration and each yielding more concentration than the previous. This way, as you pass through the jhānas, you stairstep your way to deeper and deeper levels of concentration—that is, you are becoming less and less likely to become distracted. Upon emerging from the jhānas—preferably the fourth or higher*—you begin doing an insight practice with your jhānically concentrated, indistractable mind.† This is the heart of the method the Buddha discovered—these states are not an end in and of themselves, unlike what his two teachers had taught him shortly after he'd left home to begin his spiritual quest.[7] They are simply a very useful way of preparing your mind, so you can more effectively examine reality and discover the deeper truths that lead to liberation.

---

*For example, in the *gradual training* (see http://rc.leighb.com/more/The_Gradual_Training.htm), only the four jhānas are mentioned, and insight is done after the fourth. MN 66.25 indicates that the fourth jhāna is the first of the jhānas that "belongs to the imperturbable."

† This statement is sure to be quite controversial. For more information on the controversy, see appendix 4, "In or Out: The Relationship between Jhāna Practice and Insight Practice."

PART ONE

Practical Jhānas

Introduction to Part One

As MENTIONED in the preface, the jhānas don't really lend themselves to "book learning." Any description of them is a general description, and any set of instructions is an averaging of what typically works for people to enable them to enter these states and move between them. But everyone's experience is unique; every person comes to practice with their own mental habits, talents, and understanding. Thus any initial instructions often need to be tuned for each person's background and talents.

Jhānas are best learned on a ten-day or longer meditation retreat where the teacher describes the states in a general fashion and describes the instructions, again in a general way. Then the students have time to try out the instructions for themselves. It is extremely beneficial on such a retreat that the students, after playing with the instructions for a number of meditation periods, each have multiple one-on-one interviews with a teacher to refine both the student's understanding and implementation of the instructions. A skilled jhāna teacher can modify the instructions as the teacher comes to understand to some degree how the student's mind works. For some students, the instruction might be to sit longer; for others, to relax more; and for still others, to not be sloppy.

But if a teacher were to go back to the whole group and report all the advice dispensed in a day's worth of interviews, the students would most likely become quite confused and probably think the teacher had become unhinged. Advice given to one student is exactly contrary to what another student needs to do, and the sum of all the advice would be a conflicting mishmash of confusion. This is why I say that the jhānas don't really lend themselves to book learning.

But here you are holding a jhāna book in your hands, presumably hoping to learn something. Certainly in reading this book you will have the opportunity to learn what the jhānas are plus also to read the general instructions for entering these states. And quite possibly you will attempt to follow these instructions either during your daily meditation period or on a longer residential retreat.

If you do try out these instructions, do so without expectations! Expectations are the worst thing you can bring on any retreat, and they are especially hindering when trying to learn jhānas. Additionally, if you are attempting to learn them from this book alone, you will not have direct feedback from a teacher of jhānas. Learning jhānas this way is not an impossible task, but it will certainly be a more difficult one.

With this caveat, let's now take a look at the jhānas as described in the suttas and at the instructions for entering them. Please remember as you go forward that what is presented here is one person's interpretations, opinions, and experiences; there are lots of other interpretations, opinions, and experiences about the jhānas these days. What I'm presenting here is my current understanding based on my own experience coupled with a close reading of the suttas.

1 The Preliminaries

Having taken up the rules of training, one trains oneself in them, seeing danger in the slightest faults. One comes to be endowed with wholesome bodily and verbal action, one's livelihood is purified, and one possesses moral discipline. One guards the doors of one's sense faculties, is endowed with mindfulness and clear comprehension, and is content. (DN 2.44)

THE *gradual training,** found in numerous suttas,[1] is the most detailed description of the practices undertaken by those who sought to follow the Buddha's path all the way to liberation. In Majjhima Nikāya 107, the layman Gaṇakamoggallāna points out to the Buddha that many disciplines† have a training that gradually progresses from one step to another and asks if such a gradual training exists in the Buddha's

* *Anupubbasikkhā*. In Ud 5.5, the Buddha says, "Just as the ocean has a gradual shelf, a gradual slope, a gradual inclination, with a sudden drop-off only after a long stretch, in the same way this Dhamma Discipline (dhamma-vinaya) has a gradual training (anupubbasikkhā), a gradual performance (anupubbakiriyā), a gradual progression (anupubbapatipadā), with a penetration to gnosis only after a long stretch." See also AN 8.19 & 20. The preliminaries of the gradual training are practices that begin the fulfillment of the noble eightfold path. For a detailed examination of the relationship between the gradual training and the noble eightfold path, see the web page "The Gradual Training and The Eightfold Path" at http://rc.leighb.com/more/The_Gradual_Training_and_The_Eightfold_Path.htm.

† The examples he gives include the steps of a palace, the brahmins, archers, and accountants (MN 107.2).

teachings. The Buddha replies that it does and describes the step-by-step process that takes one all the way to awakening, with each step relying on the previous to train the mind to make it possible to accomplish the next step. The jhānas are an integral part of this gradual training, and the steps prior to the jhānas are the preliminary steps necessary for learning the jhānas.

The first step of the gradual training is hearing the true dhamma* and gaining confidence† that there is a method, a path, that can be followed to gain something more valuable than what the world has to offer. The Buddha didn't require belief—only a willingness to "come and see for yourself."[2]

The next step is building the foundation upon which all that follows stands: sīla, moral discipline, ethical behavior. The major ethical practice is the keeping of the precepts—227 for monks, 311 for nuns, but only 5 for lay people:

- To refrain from killing living beings,
- To refrain from taking that which is not given,
- To refrain from committing sexual misconduct,
- To refrain from wrong speech,
- To refrain from intoxicants.

These training rules are designed to enable you to lead a life that doesn't intentionally cause harm to others or to yourself. This moral discipline includes how you earn your livelihood as well as your relationships with family, friends, and strangers. Without this moral discipline as a foundation, none of the subsequent steps will be truly effective, and

* *Dhamma* means both the teaching of the Buddha and "the way things truly are."

† *Saddhā,* usually translated as "faith" but perhaps more accurately as "confidence."

progress on the spiritual path ceases. For example, ethical behavior serves as a foundation for generating concentration by creating a life where there are not so many things you might feel remorse or worry about. For a more detailed discussion of the five precepts for lay people, see the web page "The Precepts" at http://rc.leighb.com/more/The_Precepts.htm.

You must also "guard the doors of the sense faculties" lest "evil unwholesome states assail" you.[3] This does not mean you don't look, you don't hear, and so forth; it means you do not get carried away by what you see, hear, sense, and cognize. Can you walk past a bakery, with its door open (of course), smell the wonderful aroma of the goods on offer, enjoy that smell, and yet not be tempted into entering and buying something? That's guarding the door of the nose faculty. The senses are totally necessary for navigating our environment—but they are not an amusement park, at least not if you are intent on developing the higher mind needed for liberation. It's perfectly OK to enjoy the pleasures that come via the senses—but don't let your enjoyment of them lead you to becoming even more entangled in the world of delusion. It's perfectly OK to respond to unpleasant sense contacts by dealing appropriately with the situation. But in neither case should the sense contacts lead to craving and clinging; if they do, then the sense doors are unguarded, and progress on the spiritual path is hindered.

It's also necessary to develop habitual mindfulness. We translate the word *sati* as "mindfulness," but we need to keep in mind that it is etymologically related to the Sanskrit *smṛti,* which means "memory." So being mindful means to remember. And what are we to remember? Be here, now. Pay attention to what's actually going on in the present moment, in the place where you are currently located. Now, this doesn't mean you should never plan for the future or learn from the past. But it does mean when doing so, you need to know that is what you are intending to do. In the gradual training, the Buddha suggests that you pay attention to your bodily activities throughout the day. When you are attempting to learn jhānas, this unrelenting mindfulness is the most useful of all the practices[4] given in the Satipaṭṭhāna Suttas. This practice itself won't generate sufficient concentration to enter a jhāna—but it will make it much more likely that any method that you do undertake to generate such concentration is actually effective.*

The last of the preliminary practices that occurs in the gradual training is being content with little. We unfortunately live in a culture that says that any less-than-perfect situation can be remedied by obtaining more of something—usually more of whatever the person doing the saying is selling. But the spiritual path is not about acquiring anything—it's all about letting go. There's nothing to get; there's everything to let go of. In general, throughout the two and a half thousand years of Buddhism, the jhānas were not considered a topic to be taught to lay people simply because it was believed their lives were far too busy to be able to undertake the meditation training necessary in order to learn the jhānas. But we now live in a culture with a huge opportunity for leisure, at least for some people. But we also have an unprecedented opportunity to fill up that leisure time with toys, entertainment, and other things that distract us from practice. A lay person does need more than three robes and a begging bowl, but a lay person in this culture absolutely does not need everything the culture has to offer. Leading a simple life makes it far easier to dedicate time for the practice that is necessary to progress on the spiritual path. Leading a simple life makes it easier to lead a life free from intentional harming. Leading a simple life makes it easier to abandon the five hindrances† that prevent you from entering the jhānas. Leading

* See the following chapter on access concentration for information on generating sufficient concentration to enter the jhānas.

† See the web page "Abandoning the Five Hindrances" at http://rc.leighb.com/more/Abandoning_the_Five_Hindrances.htm for more information on the hindrances.

a simple life is living more in harmony with the limited resources available to all who live on our very crowded planet.

These four preliminary practices of keeping the precepts, guarding the senses, maintaining mindfulness, and being content with little are "off-the-cushion" practices that you need to make the four cornerstones of your basic way of life. Without the support of these practices, meditation "on the cushion" usually proceeds in fits and starts, if it proceeds at all. For learning jhānas, it really is necessary to have a quality daily on-the-cushion meditation practice worthy of the word *daily,* hopefully of at least forty-five minutes and preferably an hour or more. These four practices go a long way to making that possible.

2 Access Concentration

When one sees that these five hindrances have been abandoned within himself, gladness arises. (DN 2.76)

KEY PALI WORDS:

sutta discourse, teaching
samādhi indistractability, concentration

ON ANY GIVEN RETREAT where jhānas are taught, some people will experience jhānas; some will not. The likelihood of you experiencing a jhāna is inversely proportional to the amount of desire you have for it. After all, the instructions given by the Buddha for practicing the jhānas begin, "Quite secluded from sense desire, secluded from unwholesome states of mind, one enters and remains in the first jhāna" (DN 2.77). In order to experience a jhāna, it is necessary to generate such seclusion, but actively desiring to experience a jhāna is not being secluded from the unwholesome mind state of craving. The setting aside of unwholesome mind states is known as *abandoning the hindrances.* There are five of these hindrances, usually listed as sense desire, ill will, sloth and torpor, restlessness and remorse, and doubt. They could also be listed as wanting, aversion, too little energy, too much energy, and doubt. The overcoming of these five unwholesome states of mind is the same as generating access concentration.

The Pali phrase *upacāra-samādhi,* which we translate as "access concentration," does not appear in the suttas.* But it certainly is a useful concept when discussing jhāna practice. The phrase *access concentration* means concentration strong enough to provide access to the jhānas. It is distinguished from momentary concentration (khaṇika-samādhi), which is less concentrated than access concentration, and from fixed or one-pointed concentration (appanā-samādhi), which is the stronger concentration associated with the jhānas.

We could define *access concentration* as concentration strong enough that no hindrances arise. More practically, we can define *access concentration* as being fully with the meditation object, and if there are thoughts, they are wispy and in the background and don't pull you away into distraction. The general method for generating access concentration is to put your attention on a suitable meditation object,† and when your attention wanders off, gently bring it back. Keep doing this until the distractions fade away and your attention on the object is unwavering.

This recognition that you've become distracted and the returning your attention to the meditation object should be done without becoming upset that your mind has wandered off yet again. We are the progeny of countless generations of ancestors who had to not become totally fixated on what they were doing. Those who did become fixated didn't notice a predator, got eaten, and didn't reproduce. What we are trying to do goes against millions of years of evolution. Having a wandering mind is just how we are constructed. So it's no big deal when your mind wanders off; you should actually consider it a victory that you noticed it wandered, rather than a defeat that it did its natural thing of wandering.

---

* The phrase *upacāra-samādhi* appears in the *Visuddhimagga,* where it occurs quite frequently.

† For more information on suitable meditation objects, please see below and also see appendix 3, "Access Concentration Methods."

In fact it is extremely helpful if you intentionally relax when you notice you've become distracted, and then gently reestablish attention on your meditation object. The mind state you are aiming to create could well be called *relaxed diligence.*

It is not helpful to force your mind to remain fixed on the meditation object. It's not that this cannot be done; it's that doing so will generate a mind so tense and tight that it will not have the relaxed diligence necessary for entering the jhānas. The strategy is to place your attention on the meditation object and then be diligent about recognizing when you have become distracted. Drop the distraction; it might be helpful to label the distraction with a one-word label. Labeling helps you disidentify with the thought stream and provides insight into where your mind habitually goes when it becomes distracted. Just remember that the first label that comes to mind is always correct—spend zero energy trying to find the "perfect" label. Then—very important—relax, and return your attention to your meditation object.

If you are paying close attention to the content of your distractions, you will notice that most distractions fall into one (or more) of the hindrance categories. Sometimes all it takes is just being persistent in returning to the meditation object for these hindrances to drop away. But sometimes a hindrance (or hindrances) turns out to be quite sticky. The five hindrances are discussed in detail on the web page "Abandoning the Five Hindrances" at http://rc.leighb.com/more/Abandoning_the_Five_Hindrances.htm, and general methods for working with each of these hindrances are discussed there.

If you have an especially persistent, recurring hindrance, the general methods may not work. Sometimes it helps to give that particular distraction a funny name—like maybe "Rumpelstiltskin." Then you can dialogue with it when it shows up: "It's you again, Rumpelstiltskin. Well, this is not a good time for you to be showing up; please go away!"

Giving it a funny name robs it of some of its power. Talking to it like a petulant child also weakens its hold.

If you are craving to experience a jhāna, you have the hindrance of wanting. You have to set aside such craving—those expectations—to be able to enter the jhāna. Setting aside expectations is certainly easier said than done. The best advice I can give you is to refrain from what Ayya Khema called "result thinking." Don't focus on what you hope or think or expect should happen. Ayya offered a simile that you might find helpful. Suppose you want to drive from your home to, for example, a retreat center many hours away. Suppose someone gives you excellent directions. If the directions start out by saying something like, "When you get to the end of your street, turn right. When you get to such and such a highway, turn left," it does you no good to start looking for the retreat center as you drive down your street toward the first turn. In order to use the directions properly, you don't focus on the destination; you determine where you currently are and what you'll need to do next when you arrive at the place where you change from what you are doing now to something new. This is exactly how to approach learning the jhānas. Gain an understanding of the directions. Determine where you currently are and what "landmark" to look for so that you will know when to take the next step. Don't focus on, or even think about, the destination.

The method for entering the jhānas begins with generating access concentration. You begin by sitting in a comfortable, upright position. It needs to be comfortable, because if there is too much pain, the unwholesome mental state of aversion will naturally develop. You may be able to sit in a way that looks really good, but if your knees are killing you, there will be pain and you will not experience any jhānas. So you need to find some way to sit that is comfortable. But it also needs to be upright and alert, because that tends to get your energy going in a beneficial way that keeps you awake. On the other hand, if you are too comfortable, you might be overcome with sloth and torpor, which is also an unwholesome mental state that of course is totally useless for entering the jhānas.

So the first prerequisite for entering the jhānas is to put your body in a position that you can just leave it in for the length of the meditation period without having to move. If you have back problems or some other obstacle that prevents you from sitting upright, then you need to find some other alert position you can maintain comfortably.

Now, this is not to say you cannot move. It may be that you have taken a position and you discover something: "My knee is killing me; I have to move because there is too much aversion." If you have to move, you have to move. Just be mindful of the moving. The intention to move will be there before the movement. Notice that intention; then move very mindfully, and then resettle yourself into the new position, and notice the mind working to get back to that place of calm that it had before you moved. It is very important that you not move unmindfully.

This process encourages you to find a position where you don't have to move, because you'll notice the amount of disturbance that even a slight movement generates. And in order to become concentrated enough to have the jhānas manifest, you need a very calm mind. Other things that can be useful after getting settled into your sitting posture are discussed in appendix 2, "Helpful Things to Do at the Beginning and End of Each Meditation Period."

Generating access concentration can be done in a number of ways. This chapter and the next one will mostly talk about generating it using the breath, a practice known as *ānāpānasati.* The first word of this Pali compound, *ānāpāna,* means "in-breath and out-breath," while the word *sati* means "mindfulness." The practice is therefore "mindfulness of breathing."* When practicing ānāpānasati, you put your attention on the

---

* For more detailed instruction for working with mindfulness of breathing, see appendix 3.

physical sensations associated with breathing. It is extremely important to not control the breath in any way—just pay attention to the naturally occurring breathing. If you control the breath, it does make it easier to not become distracted. But it makes it too easy, and you won't generate sufficient concentration to enter the jhānas.

It is probably better if you can observe the physical sensations at the nostrils or on the area between the nose and the upper lip, rather than at the abdomen or elsewhere. It is better because it is more difficult to do; therefore, you have to concentrate more. Since you are trying to generate access concentration, you take something that is doable, though not terribly easy to do, and then you do it. When noticing the natural, uncontrolled breath at the nose, you have to pay attention very carefully.

In doing so you will notice the tactile sensations, and then your mind will wander off. Then you'll bring it back, and it will wander off; then you'll bring it back, and it will wander off. Eventually though—maybe not the next time you sit in meditation, maybe not even tomorrow or next week or next month, but eventually—you'll find that the mind locks onto the breath. You're really with the breath, and the mind is not wandering off. Any thoughts you have are wispy and in the background. The thoughts might be something like, "Wow, I'm really with the breath now," as opposed to, "When I get to Hawaii, the first thing I'm going to do is . . . ."

When the thoughts are just slight, when they're not really pulling you away and you're fully with the sensations of the breath, knowing each in-breath and each out-breath—this is the sign that you've arrived at access concentration. Whatever method you use to generate access concentration, the sign that you've gotten to access concentration is that you are fully present with the object of meditation. So if you are doing mettā (loving-kindness meditation), you're just fully there with the feeling of mettā; you're not getting distracted. If you're doing the body-sweeping practice, you're fully there with the sensations in the body as you sweep your attention over the body.* You're not thinking extraneous thoughts; you're not planning; you're not worrying; you're not angry; you're not wanting something. You are just fully there with whatever your object is.

As you start to become concentrated, you might notice various lights and colors even though your eyes are closed. These are signs that you are starting to get concentrated. There is generally nothing useful that can be done with them—just ignore them. When you actually do get quite concentrated, the random blobs and laser light shows will disappear. They might be replaced by a diffused white light, which is a sign of good concentration. It always appears for some people, it never appears for others, and many people find it sometimes appears and sometimes does not appear. But again, there's nothing you need to do with that sign either—it's just a sign. When you drive into a town and see a sign saying, "Entering Citytown," you don't need to stop your car, get out, uproot the sign, and toss it in the trunk of your car; you don't need to do anything with the sign—it is just providing information about where you are. The diffused white light is a sign saying, "Entering Concentrationville." Nice; just stay focused on your meditation object!

* For more detailed instructions for working with mettā and the body sweep as access methods, see appendix 3.

3 Entering the Jhānas

From gladness, rapture arises. (DN 2.76)

KEY PALI WORDS:

samādhi	indistractability, concentration
pāmojja	gladness, worldly joy
pīti	glee, rapture, euphoria, ecstasy, delight
sukha	happiness, joy

If your practice is ānāpānasati—mindfulness of breathing—there may possibly arise additional signs to indicate you have arrived at access concentration. You may discover that the breath becomes very subtle; instead of a normal breath, you notice you are breathing very shallowly. It may even seem that you've stopped breathing altogether. These are signs that you've likely arrived at access concentration. If the breath gets very shallow, and particularly if it feels like you've stopped breathing, the natural thing to do is to take a nice, deep breath and get it going again. Wrong! This will tend to weaken your concentration. By taking that nice deep breath, you decrease the strength of your concentration. Just stay with that shallow breathing. It's OK. You don't need a lot of oxygen because you are very quiet, both physically and mentally.

If the breath gets very, very subtle, or if it disappears entirely, instead of taking a deep breath, shift your attention away from the breath to a pleasant sensation. This is the key thing. You notice the breath until you arrive at and sustain access concentration, and then you let go of the breath and shift your attention to a pleasant sensation, preferably a pleasant physical sensation. There is not much point in trying to notice the breath that has gotten extremely subtle or has disappeared completely—there's nothing left to notice.

If you arrive at access concentration (which, remember, is defined as being fully with the object of meditation and not becoming distracted even if there are wispy, background thoughts) and can maintain this access concentration for five to ten to fifteen minutes, you can also shift your attention away from the breath to a pleasant sensation even if the breath is still distinct. Whether you shift to the pleasant sensation because your breath has gotten too subtle or because you've been at access concentration "long enough," you will need a good bit of concentration to continuously notice a pleasant sensation. A mildly pleasant physical sensation somewhere in your body is not nearly as exciting as the breath coming in and the breath going out. You're experiencing this mildly pleasant sensation that's just sitting there; you need to be well concentrated to stay with it.

The first question that may arise when I say, "Shift your attention to a pleasant sensation," may be "What pleasant sensation?" Well, it turns out that when you get to access concentration, the odds are quite strong that, some place in your physical being, there will be a pleasant sensation. Look at most any statue of the Buddha: he has a faint smile on his face. That is not just for artistic purposes; it is there for teaching purposes. Smile when you meditate, because once you reach access concentration, you only have to shift your attention one inch to find a pleasant sensation.

Now, when I tell you, "Smile when you meditate," your reaction might be "I don't feel like smiling when I meditate." I know this because when they told me to smile when I meditated, my reaction was "I don't feel like smiling." OK, so you don't feel like smiling. Nonetheless, if you put a fake smile on your face when you start meditating, and keep putting it back on if it falls off, by the time you arrive at access concentration, the smile will feel genuine.

If you can smile when you meditate, it works very well for generating a pleasant sensation to focus upon once you've established access concentration; but actually, smiling seems to only work for about a quarter of the students I've worked with. Too many people in this culture have been told, "Smile whether you feel like it or not." And so now when I tell you, "Smile whether you feel like it or not," maybe your reaction is "No, I'm not gonna do that." OK, so you don't smile when you meditate. You'll have to find some other pleasant sensation.

Pleasant sensations can occur pretty much anywhere. The most common place that people find pleasant sensations when they've established access concentration is in the hands. What you want to do with your hands when you meditate is put them in a nice position in which you can just leave them. The traditional posture is one hand holding the other, with the thumbs lightly touching. This is a quite excellent posture because it has a side effect of moving the shoulders back and lining up your spine nicely. When the hands are held like this, many people find that eventually there is a nice, tingly pleasant sensation that appears in the hands. But you can also put your hands in all sorts of other positions—just place them however appeals to you. After you've been "long enough" in access concentration, if you notice that there's a nice pleasant feeling in the hands, drop the attention on the breath and focus entirely on the pleasantness of that sensation.

Another common place people find a pleasant sensation is in the heart center, particularly if they're using mettā—loving-kindness—meditation as the access method. Just shift your attention to the pleasantness of that sensation. Other places people find pleasant sensations include the third eye, the top of the head, the shoulders—actually, you name a body part, and I've had some student find a pleasant sensation there that they were able to focus on long enough for the first jhāna to arise. It does not matter where the pleasant sensation manifests; what matters is that there is a pleasant sensation and you're able to put your attention on it and—now here comes the really hard part—do nothing else.

At first, what's most likely to occur is that either your mind wanders away from the subtle pleasant sensation or the pleasant sensation itself goes away. If your mind wanders away, as soon as you notice this, return immediately to the pleasant sensation. But if this wandering away is happening repeatedly, it's a sign of insufficient concentration; therefore, return to the mindfulness of breathing or whatever other access method you were using, regenerate access concentration, and stay longer in access concentration before once again turning your attention to the pleasant sensation.

If the pleasant sensation goes away, you don't really have any other choice than to return to your previous access method. The disappearance of the pleasant sensation is a sure sign of insufficient concentration. Again, regenerate access concentration, and stay longer in access concentration before once again turning your attention to the pleasant sensation.

It's also very important to let go of the breath when you make the shift to the pleasant sensation. The breath (or other meditation object) is the key to get you in—"in" being synonymous with establishing strong enough access concentration. When you come home from work, you pull out your key, you open the door to your home, and you go in. You don't then wander around with the key still in your hand—you put it back in your pocket or purse or on some table. You're not cooking dinner or watching TV with the key still in your hand! The key has done its job, and you let it go. It's exactly the same with the breath or other meditation object. Totally let go of it, and focus entirely on the pleasant sensation. Of course, this is easier said than done—you've struggled for a long time to stay locked onto the breath, and now that you've finally managed to do so, the first thing you are told is to stop doing that. But that's the way it is—if you want to experience jhānas, it's going to be necessary to totally give yourself to fully enjoying the pleasantness of the pleasant sensation.

So you've found the pleasant sensation and fully shifted your attention to that pleasant sensation. You now observe the pleasantness of the pleasant sensation and do nothing else. If you can do that, the pleasant sensation will begin to grow in intensity; it will become stronger. This will not happen in a linear way. At first, nothing happens. Then it'll grow a little bit and then grow a little bit more and then hang out and grow a little bit more.... And then eventually, it will suddenly take off and take you into what is obviously an altered state of consciousness.

In this altered state of consciousness, you will be overcome with rapture... euphoria... ecstasy... delight. These are all English words that are used to translate the Pali word *pīti.* Perhaps the best English word for *pīti* is "glee." Pīti is a primarily physical sensation that sweeps you powerfully into an altered state. But pīti is not solely physical; as the suttas say, "On account of the presence of pīti there is mental exhilaration."[1] In addition to the physical energy and mental exhilaration, the pīti will be accompanied by an emotional sensation of joy and happiness. The Pali word for this joy/happiness is *sukha,* the opposite of dukkha (pain, suffering). And, if you can remain undistractedly focused on this experience of pīti and sukha, that is the first jhāna.

So to summarize the method for entering the first jhāna: You sit in a nice comfortable upright position and generate access concentration by placing and eventually maintaining your attention on a single meditation object. When access concentration is firmly established, then you shift your attention from the breath (or whatever your meditation object is) to a pleasant sensation, preferably a pleasant physical sensation. You put your attention on that sensation, and maintain your attention on that sensation, and do nothing else.

The hard part is the "do nothing else" part. You put your attention on the pleasant sensation, and nothing happens, so you might think to yourself, "He said something was supposed to happen." No, I did not say to make comments about experiencing the pleasant sensation. Or, you might put your attention on the pleasant sensation, and it starts to increase, so you think, "Oh! Oh! Something's happening!" No, don't do that—that will only make it go away. Or it comes up just a little bit, and then it stops, and you sort of try and help it. Nope, none of this works. Just simply observe the pleasant sensation.

You must become totally immersed in the pleasantness of the pleasant sensation. And I mean by this just what I say: the pleasantness of the pleasant sensation—the quality of the sensation that enables you to determine that it is pleasant, rather than unpleasant or neither. It's not the location of the pleasant sensation nor its intensity nor its duration. It's not whether the pleasant sensation is increasing or decreasing or staying the same. Just focus entirely upon the pleasant aspect of the pleasant sensation, and the jhāna will arise on its own. Now, admittedly, the sensation will be located in a particular area, and your attention will be aimed at that area. That's fine; just don't get caught up in the location; stay with just enjoying the pleasantness of the pleasant sensation.

All you can do is set up the conditions for the jhāna to arise, by cultivating a calm and quiet mind focused on pleasantness. And then just let go—be that calm, quiet mind focused on pleasantness and enjoy the pleasantness—and the jhāna will appear. Any attempt to do anything more does not work. You actually have to become a human being, as opposed to a human doing. You have to become a being that is simply focused on a pleasant sensation that is simply existing, and then the jhāna comes all on its own.

What you are attempting to do is set up a positive feedback loop. An example of a positive feedback loop is that awful noise a speaker will make if a microphone is held too close to it. What's happening is that the ambient noise in the room goes into the microphone, is amplified by the amplifier, and comes out the speaker louder. It then reenters the microphone, gets amplified even more, comes out louder still, goes into the microphone yet again, and so on. You are trying to do exactly the same thing, except, rather than a positive feedback loop of noise, you are attempting to generate a positive feedback loop of pleasure. You hold your attention on a pleasant sensation. That feels nice, adding a bit more pleasure to your overall experience. That addition is also pleasurable, adding even more pleasure, and so on, until, instead of getting a horrible noise, you get an explosion of pleasure that goes by the names of *pīti* and *sukha.*

Imagine that your mind is like a still pool—still because of the access concentration. Now drop in a pebble of pleasure. The ripples go out to the "sides of your skull" and bounce off and come back together. When they come together they reinforce each other, generating taller waves. But because this is not a real, physical system, if you don't disturb the system, the ripples stay taller and don't die out; they keep bouncing off the sides and reinforcing each other more and more. This is what we are after. But it requires that you not stir the water in the pool; doing so would spoil the bouncing and reinforcing effect, and the system would not keep generating higher waves.*

* This of course is in no way related to what's actually happening from a neuroscientific perspective—it's only an imaginative way of expressing the idea of what is to be accomplished by the quiet focus on the pleasantness of the pleasant sensation.

These are the instructions for entering the first jhāna. But don't expect the necessary concentration to show up anytime soon. In fact, don't expect anything! Expectations are the absolute worst things you can bring on a retreat, and they are equally detrimental when practicing while not on retreat. Simply do the meditation method. And when access concentration arises, recognize it, sustain it "long enough," and then shift your attention to a pleasant sensation. Don't try to do the jhānas. You can't. All you can do is generate the conditions out of which the jhānas can arise. Recognize when you've established these conditions, and then patiently wait for the jhāna to come find you.

Possible Problems Associated with Attempting to Enter the Jhānas

> *It is not easy, living the household life, to live the fully-perfected holy life, purified and polished like a conch-shell. (DN 2.41)*

The path to experiencing the jhānas is not an easy one. There are a number of ways for things to go wrong, a number of ways to work very hard and yet not experience any jhānas. This section looks at some of the difficulties that might be encountered along the way to learning the jhānas.

The most common problem encountered is, rather obviously, insufficient concentration. This can arise from a number of different causes. The most common cause is what I term "jumping too soon." Someone manages to follow a few breaths in a row and immediately switches to some pleasant sensation. The concentration generated by "a few breaths in a row" is far too little to sustain attention on the pleasant sensation. The student becomes distracted and/or the pleasant sensation disappears.

Similarly, someone switches to a pleasant sensation as soon as one appears. They have not established access concentration and soon become distracted and are unable to maintain focus on the pleasant sensation or the pleasant sensation disappears.

Similarly, someone does actually generate access concentration but almost immediately switches to a pleasant sensation, maybe just as soon as genuine access concentration is recognized. But because the access concentration is not strong enough, the student becomes distracted or the pleasant sensation disappears.

The opposite problem arises a good bit less frequently, but it does occur. Someone generates quite good access concentration but keeps thinking that it's not good enough and never lets go of the access method in order to switch to the pleasant sensation.

Much more likely is that someone generates quite good access concentration, switches to the pleasant sensation, but grows impatient. The impatience can lead to mentally commenting about how it's not working, which leads to distraction. The impatience can lead to trying to make the pīti arise by "doing" something rather than just *being* with the experience of the pleasant sensation.

All of the above problems are minor in the sense that they are fairly easily dealt with by tuning the student's patience—not too little, not too much, middle way. Learning the jhānas is very definitely a trial-and-error process—with lots of errors along the way. This is why it's good to undertake jhāna training while on an extended residential meditation retreat. A skilled jhāna teacher can, one hopes, easily recognize any of the above problems and offer suggestions to correct them—and the student has plenty of opportunities to try, try again.

Another somewhat commonly occurring problem when working with mindfulness of breathing is that someone gets nicely concentrated, the breath gets quite subtle, and then it feels like they just have to take a breath. Unless you are intentionally stifling your breath, you probably don't really have to take a breath. After all, most of the breaths you've taken during your life have not been taken under your conscious control. Your body knows how much oxygen you need and knows what to do to get it. If you can just ignore that feeling and trust that your system can take care of itself, that's probably best. But for people who get the feeling that they just have to take a breath, this suggestion seldom seems to work. More likely what is going to work is to take a slightly deeper breath. That will cause a slight setback on your way toward deep enough concentration, but not nearly as much as taking a big, deep breath. So take the slightly deeper breath, and return to letting the breath function automatically. Be patient—you might have to do several cycles of this on your way to deep enough concentration for the jhānas to manifest.

A similar problem is that a deep gasp occurs unexpectedly. This is a bit harder to solve. The best thing is to notice the precursors of the automatic gasp, and when you see it is getting likely that you will soon gasp, then intentionally take a slightly deeper breath to prevent the deep gasp.

A much more serious problem is that someone generates good access concentration, but when they attempt to switch to a pleasant sensation, there is none to be found anywhere in the body. This is a much more difficult problem to remedy. A pleasant mental sensation can certainly be used as the meditation object for generating pīti—but there are two major drawbacks: the pleasant mental sensation, which is most likely an emotion, is likely to have a story connected with it that then leads to distraction, or the pleasant mental sensation is unstable and soon fades away.

If this is the problem you are dealing with, the best pleasant mental sensation to work with is the feeling of loving-kindness (mettā). If you cannot find a pleasant physical sensation after having definitely established good access concentration, switch to doing mettā practice for a few minutes. Does this generate a pleasant feeling in the area around the heart? If so, focus on that. If mettā practice generates any pleasant bodily sensation, use that. If you can stay focused on the feeling of mettā, without using words or distracting images, use the mettā feeling itself as the pleasant sensation. If mettā doesn't work for you, you can try doing gratitude practice and see if that will generate a pleasant sensation you can focus on. If gratitude doesn't work, you can try using a pleasant memory—a memory that brings a smile to your face. You are better off not planning what memory you'll use; just grab a happy one after your access concentration is well established, and see if you can sustain the happy feeling without getting caught in a story.

If the lack of a stable pleasant sensation persists, this problem may require more work than can be done during the retreat; it may require more time or a more psychological approach or both. What is sometimes going on is a persistent dysthymic-like mood. The psychological condition dysthymia has a number of typical characteristics: low drive, low self-esteem, and a low capacity for pleasure in everyday life. That may or may not be what's happening here, but raising the "capacity for pleasure in everyday life" does seem to be helpful in establishing the ability to find a pleasant bodily sensation once access concentration is established. One of the best methods for doing this is more mettā, more compassion, and more muditā (appreciative joy) practice. Also, neurologically, pīti and sukha seem to be accompanied by increased activity in the nucleus accumbens of the brain—the reward center. If your life doesn't seem to be very rewarding, then certainly changing your life so that you feel more rewarded will exercise the reward center, and this may help. Just be sure to choose wisely and wholesomely when picking activities that you hope will exercise the reward center.

Another problem that can block the arising of any jhāna is the inability to let go of attention on the breath. This may require practice over the course of a number of meditation periods. But if you are trying to focus on a pleasant sensation and on the sensations of the breath at the same time, you are obviously not focused on just one thing—which is what is required to generate access concentration. The simple solution is, of course, to *ignore the breath*. But maybe that's easier said than done. Keep trying.

Another possible solution to the above problem of not being able to let go of the breath is to find the breath itself to be pleasant. This involves a subtle shift from the physical sensations of the breath to the pleasantness of the breath. For some people, this works very well. For others, they just wind up continuing to track the breath without experiencing enough pleasantness to generate the pīti and sukha.

Another problem that some students face is fear of loss of control. It simply is not possible to enter the first jhāna and be in control during the whole experience. You have to let go and let the pīti take over. What sometimes happens is that someone generates quite good access concentration, switches to the pleasant sensation, and eventually the pleasant sensation begins morphing into pīti. And that experience can be accompanied by a sense that something unintended is happening in one's mental sphere—in other words, things are getting out of control. The fear generated in the face of this experience results in the person—intentionally or unintentionally—drawing back and shutting down the pīti, thereby blocking any jhānic experience.

If you are faced with the above reaction, the first thing to realize is that you have never actually been in control of anything ever. All that you are losing is the illusion of being in control! Jhāna practice is safe—if it were not, all the people today practicing jhānas on a regular and frequent basis would probably be dead by now. Furthermore, the Buddha highly recommended them—and he was very big on not causing harm. Now having said all this, practice of the first jhāna might be contraindicated for someone prone to seizures. There have been no studies done on this, and, as far as I know, there is no empirical evidence; I mention it only out of extreme caution. But unless you are prone to seizures, there is absolutely nothing to fear.

Now, assuring you that there is nothing to fear is probably not enough to make the fear entirely disappear. What seems to happen in these cases is that the student, feeling a bit more reassured, lets go into the out-of-control feeling a little deeper each time before intentionally or unintentionally drawing back. It's sort of like testing the waters to see if it's safe. And eventually they get so close to the pīti fully erupting that it does fully erupt, and they find themselves in the first jhāna—and still safe. The problem is then solved.

A more common problem than the preceding ones is that working with concentration—whether it is jhānic concentration, access concentration, or even a lesser form of concentration—can result in someone's unresolved psychological issues surfacing. All that energy that was being used to keep those issues at bay has now gotten quiet; all the hustle and bustle of a busy life has gone, and there is no longer the noise to drown out those issues. The arising of such psychological issues is not a bad thing; in fact, it is actually a very useful thing. But it's not a pleasant thing! However, it is much better to have these issues surface where they can be dealt with, rather than have them lurking underground doing who knows what at a subconscious or unconscious level. But the arising of these psychological issues is a distraction for sure. They often generate aversion or some other hindering quality. They can be enough of an overriding issue that they cannot be set aside and have to be dealt with skillfully and immediately. This dealing with issues may take up all of one's time and energy and not leave the quiet, undisturbed mind that is needed to enter the jhānas. But the fact that these issues are now in the open and can be dealt with is a very valuable opportunity, and the work of dealing with them can begin at once. It is not uncommon for someone on a retreat to have an extremely profitable experience because they dealt skillfully with what surfaced; in fact they often have a more useful experience than if they had just been hanging out in the jhānas. Sometimes the issues get resolved during the retreat; sometimes they even get resolved "enough" to return to jhāna practice; more often the resolving of them is a longer-term project.

A problem that appears infrequently is experiencing a headache. If this happens to you, the first thing to check is to make sure you are not crossing your eyes. "Watching the breath" is occasionally subconsciously taken too literally.

More frequently a headache is due to "stuck pīti." This type of headache is almost always in the center of the head, as opposed to off to one side, and quite frequently in the center of the forehead or near the crown of the head. It seems to arise when someone begins generating pīti but that pīti has not yet erupted. Neurologically, there have been no studies done to ascertain what's going on in this situation, but the hypothesis is that the neurotransmitter(s), which are experienced as pīti when there is a sufficient concentration of them, are being generated, but not in a sufficient enough quantity for the pīti to arise. The most effective remedy if you are experiencing this type of headache seems to be to sweep your attention up your spine from your tailbone, up and then out of your head at the spot the headache seems the strongest. Each sweep should take about a half a second, and your attention should be traveling slightly faster at the end of the sweep than at the beginning. You are not trying to move anything up your spine other than your attention. Do this 10 to 12 times, and return to your meditation. Sometimes this will clear the headache; sometimes it will trigger the onset of pīti and thereby clear the headache; sometimes it does nothing. How and why it works when it works is not known.

Luckily most of the problems described above are rare. The most common one is not allowing the access concentration to grow strong enough before shifting to a pleasant sensation—and that one has the easy remedy of patience. The second most common is some unresolved psychological issue surfacing. And although this can block access to the jhānas, it nonetheless is a valuable opportunity for growth. It seems that clearing away personal psychological issues is very helpful for preparing the mind for gaining the deeper transformative insights into the impersonal nature of reality.

4 First Jhāna

Quite secluded from sense pleasures, secluded from unwholesome states, one enters and dwells in the first jhāna, which is accompanied by thinking and examining and filled with the rapture and happiness born of seclusion. One drenches, steeps, saturates, and suffuses one's body with this rapture and happiness born of seclusion, so that there is no part of one's entire body which is not suffused by this rapture and happiness. (DN 2.77)

KEY PALI WORDS:

samādhi	indistractability, concentration
pāmojja	gladness, worldly joy
vitakka	thinking
vicāra	examining
pīti	glee, rapture
sukha	happiness/joy

THE JHĀNAS OCCUR in a large number of suttas,* not only in just the suttas that give the gradual training. The description is almost

* The jhānas are mentioned in about half the suttas of the Dīgha Nikāya and in over a third of the suttas of the Majjhima Nikāya. There is a whole saṃyutta (collection) in the Saṃyutta Nikāya on the jhānas, and they are mentioned in many additional saṃyutta suttas, as well as in many suttas in the Anguttara-Nikāya.

everywhere exactly the same. Occasionally you find it changed slightly, occasionally you find additional information given, but pretty much you find it's the exact same description over and over again. This makes sense given that suttas were preserved in an oral tradition and reciters learned particular patterns.* When a reciter got to a place in a sutta where it talked about A, the reciter recited pattern A, and when a reciter got to the part where it talked about J, the reciter recited pattern J. Thus a lot of detail and natural variability has most likely been lost.

Furthermore, the detailed instructions for the jhānas, which quite likely varied depending on the teacher and the students, really would not fit well into the oral literature. So what we have preserved for us is more like an outline. If the information in the outline was not sufficient for a student of the Buddha, the student would study with a teacher to learn the details. This and the following chapters are my interpretation of these details.† In Part Two, we'll take a more scholarly look at these details and their relationship to the words found in the suttas.

The first jhāna description starts: "Quite secluded from sense pleasures, secluded from unwholesome states, one enters and remains in the first jhāna." As mentioned previously, this seclusion from sense pleasures, seclusion from unwholesome states, refers to the abandoning of the five hindrances, the five mental states that hinder progress on the spiritual path. The method for setting them aside is generating access concentration. Access concentration gets you to the point where, if there are thoughts occurring, they are wispy and in the background and

---

* Pericopes: In rhetoric, a *pericope* is a "stock passage" of text that forms one coherent unit or thought, suitable for public reciting or reading from a text, now usually referring to sacred scripture. For more information about periscopes, see Anālayo, *Comparative Study,* 16–17.

† There are multiple interpretations of the sutta descriptions of the jhānas. See for example http://leighb.com/jhanantp.htm.

they are not pulling you away into distraction. At that level of concentration, these hindrances will not arise.

In the gradual training, just before the description of the jhānas, frequently the suttas say, "When one sees that the five hindrances have been abandoned within oneself, gladness arises." In other words, when you generate access concentration, the gladness referred to here (the Pali word is *pāmojja*) is the mental state generated by the pleasant sensation that you're to put your attention on after having stabilized and deepened access concentration. With the hindrances out of the way, this is a pretty nice state. "From gladness, rapture arises": rapture (pīti) being the primary ingredient of the first jhāna. The unwavering attention on the gladness (the enjoyment of the pleasant sensation) generates the pīti, which is both the gateway to and the primary component of the first jhāna.

Then the suttas describe the qualities of the first jhāna, "which is accompanied by thinking and examining and is filled with the rapture and happiness born of seclusion." These four qualities are often identified as factors of the first jhāna. The later commentaries assert that there are five factors, but the suttas only mention the four qualities, which are thinking and examining, rapture and happiness. The thinking and examining are translations of the Pali words *vitakka* and *vicāra*. The commentaries interpret these words to mean initial and sustained attention on the meditation object. Now, it's very true that in order to do any sort of concentrated meditation, you need initial and sustained attention on the meditation object. However, this doesn't appear to be what the Buddha is talking about: in the suttas, *vitakka* and *vicāra* always and only refer to thinking.* When you generate access concentration and sustain it, there may be still a bit of thinking in the background—which

* See chapter 11, "Vitakka and Vicāra," for more information.

can basically be ignored. This background thinking persists in the first jhāna and is what is being referred to by the words *vitakka* and *vicāra.*

As mentioned in the previous chapter, the move from access concentration to the first jhāna is to shift your attention to a pleasant sensation and stay with that as your object of attention, ignoring any background thinking. If you can stay with your undistracted attention on the pleasant sensation, then pīti will arise. The pīti, being the physical release of pleasant, exhilarating energy, could be anywhere from mild to quite intense. It can be finger-in-the-electrical-socket intense; it can be so intense that it's not even pleasurable. And hopefully the pīti is accompanied by sukha, which is an emotional state of joy, happiness. Both pīti and sukha are required in order for the experience to be classified as the first jhāna. And most likely, the experience brings a big grin to your face. The first jhāna is enough of an altered state that if you think some experience perhaps might be the first jhāna, it probably isn't—there's an unmistakable quality to the arising of pīti and sukha that lets you know for certain that something quite different is happening.

To remain in the first jhāna, stay focused on the experience of pīti and sukha. In the Poṭṭhapāda Sutta (DN 9.10) we find, "Having reached the first jhāna, one remains in it. . . . At that time there is present a true but subtle perception of pīti and sukha born of seclusion, and one becomes one who is conscious of this pīti and sukha." The phrase "one who is conscious of this pīti and sukha" tells us that our object of attention is now the experience of pīti and sukha.

At first, it's really not easy to tell the pīti and sukha apart. This experience, this energy, this state, has come over you and grabbed your full attention. It is not readily apparent that there is an emotional component apart from the physical component, nor is it necessary to distinguish the two—yet. The experience may be much more one of pervasive pīti-sukha than one composed of intermingled distinct pīti and distinct sukha. As mentioned above, you may also find that there is a bit of thinking going on in the background. That's OK—it's the vitakka and vicāra, the thinking and examining, which are still lurking in the background of the first jhāna. Don't get distracted by the background thinking; stay focused on the experience of pīti-sukha. Maintaining this pīti-sukha experience and the focus on it constitutes the first jhāna.

You'll notice that the jhāna description says that the pīti and sukha are "born of seclusion." In other words, they arise from the fact that you have become secluded from the hindrances by gaining access concentration. Access concentration, or seclusion, is what generates the pleasant sensation, and unwavering attention on it generates the pīti and sukha. It does not mean, as some people incorrectly say, that you have to go and seclude yourself in the forest. You just have to seclude your mind from the hindrances, and this is what will generate the pīti and sukha.

Once you have arrived at the state where the pīti and the sukha are sustained, the suttas say: "One drenches, steeps, saturates, and suffuses one's body with this rapture and happiness born of seclusion, so that there is no part of one's entire body which is not suffused by this rapture and happiness." When you're initially in the first jhāna, the pīti energy may seem to run up the spine and involve the back of the body, upper torso, and head more than anyplace else. Or maybe it's just in the upper torso and head. Either of these is fine. Actually, when you are first learning, just get the pīti-sukha going and sustained; it doesn't matter where it's located or that it's not yet throughout the body. Spreading it throughout the whole body is a more advanced practice. The pīti-sukha will probably feel like it's centered more in the area of the face. Sometimes it's most prevalent in the head, sometimes in the spine, but in general, it's principally in the upper body area around the face. Then when you get skilled enough to stabilize the first jhāna, you'll find that it is possible to move the energy into the arms and legs so that your whole body is filled with it. The method is to just move your attention from the location where the pīti feels the strongest to an area where it does not seem to be occurring, such as down an arm. You are not trying to move the energy; you are only moving your attention. Bring your attention back to the place where the pīti felt strong, and then notice whether the energy spread to the area where you moved your attention. Continue doing this in a gentle, unhurried way until the pīti and sukha fill the whole body. But please remember: this is an advanced practice; don't worry about trying to spread the pīti and sukha immediately. Just get the pīti and sukha going, and see whether you can sustain them and sustain your attention on them.

For each of the first four jhānas, we have a simile. For this first one we find:

> Suppose a skilled bath attendant or his apprentice were to pour soap flakes into a metal basin, sprinkle them with water and knead them into a ball, so that the ball of soap flakes would be pervaded by moisture, encompassed by moisture, suffused by moisture inside and out and yet would not trickle. In the same way one drenches, steeps, saturates and suffuses one's body with the rapture and happiness born of seclusion, so that there is no part of one's body that is not suffused by rapture and happiness. (DN 2.78)

We have here a picture of what life was like at the time of the Buddha. You didn't go to the store and buy a bar of soap. You had your skilled bath attendant or his apprentice get a metal basin and pour soap flakes into it, pour water in, and then mix the soap flakes and the water until he had a ball of soap.

This picture matches quite well the frenetic energy of the first jhāna.

The first jhāna is not a calm, peaceful state. Its energy is pretty intense, and this simile gives a fairly good idea of the lack of calm and of the frenetic energy that is present in the first jhāna. There's an effervescent quality to the first jhāna that can also be gleaned from the simile. The particulars of the simile are that the soap flakes are like your body, and the water is like the pīti and sukha, which go throughout the body so that they are fully everywhere. As I've said, this occurs as you become more skilled. Your first goal should be to get the pīti and sukha going, and then sustain them. Once you are skilled at that, then hang out in the first jhāna and begin to play with it as described below, and finally see about moving it throughout the various parts of your body.

Another thing you can do in the first jhāna is play with the intensity level of the pīti. Once you've gotten to the point where you can stabilize it, see if you can decrease the level of intensity of the pīti and then bring it back up. You are, so to speak, finding a sort of mental volume control for the pīti. It is easier to bring the pīti down and then back up than it is to try to pump it up higher still. Besides, the pīti may be quite intense, and pumping it up higher may not be something you want to do. The method for decreasing the volume on the pīti is to give it a little less energy, a little less attention. Don't pay quite as much attention to it, and it will begin to decrease. Once it comes down, put your attention fully back on it, and bring it back up. Once you are skilled in playing with the intensity level of the pīti, you can try to shut it off suddenly and completely, followed by immediately bringing it back. These skills will begin to give you mastery of the pīti that will be useful for learning the second and third jhānas.

The length of time you'll want to stay in the first jhāna is inversely proportional to the intensity of the pīti. In other words, if the pīti is very strong, you probably won't want to stay there very long. Half a minute or so might be sufficient, maybe even less than that if the pīti is seriously intense. If the pīti is not so very strong, then you might want to stay there five to ten minutes. The timing just depends on the strength of the pīti.

Pīti comes in a number of "grades." It can show up as momentary pīti, which is like a shiver and then it's gone. It can be minor pīti, which is a little tingly feeling that's sustaining but not very strong and is more or less in the background. Minor pīti can also show up as gentle, involuntary rocking as you meditate. You might experience showering pīti, which is when you get a burst of pīti and then it's gone, another burst and then that's gone—the pīti is arising but not sustaining. It can be uplifting pīti that makes your hair stand on end. It can give you a sense that you are levitating when it's really strong. I have had several students report opening their eyes to see whether they were indeed levitating. I'm afraid no one has ever reported getting off the ground. However, uplifting pīti can make you sit up very straight. The fifth kind of pīti is what I usually refer to as *full-blown pīti.* The correct translation is "all-pervasive pīti." This is the pīti that is everywhere. It's present, it's sustained, and you experience it throughout your body. It's the pīti necessary for the first jhāna; the other four types are pre-jhāna pīti, and they may or may not show up as you progress toward access concentration and then to the arising of the first jhāna.[1]

Pīti can manifest as rocking or swaying, or it can be very intense so that you are actually vibrating to the point where it is visible to others. It can manifest as heat and get very, very warm. Hopefully it has a pleasant aspect to it. Most often, it manifests as an upward rush of energy, often centered up the spine. I've talked with people who practice kundalini yoga, and it seems that pīti is the same energy. I've talked with people who practice *tummo,*[2] which is the Tibetan practice of generating heat, and I was told that this practice also involves generating the same sort of energy. It's a known, widespread phenomenon that is used in different ways. Here it is used to grab your attention and take you into a concentrated state due to it being so strong that it is easy to put your attention on it and absorb into the experience. The arising of pīti also has the nice side effect (for most people) of generating sukha, and, as we'll see, the sukha is the principal component of the second and third jhānas, as well as being a necessary part of the first jhāna.

So, you hang out in the first jhāna for a bit, depending on how strong the pīti is: if it is very strong, a half minute or so; if it is weaker, then maybe up to five or ten minutes. It should also be mentioned that when pīti first arrives, you may not have any control over the strength of it. It may come on ridiculously strong, or it may come on weak. I never know when talking with someone about their experiences in access concentration and working with the pleasant sensation just what is going to happen when the pīti finally does arrive, so just go with whatever shows up. The reason it can come on very strong the first time is somewhat like a can of soda pop. If you shake it for four or five days and then pop the top, it goes all over. The good news is that the next time pīti comes on, it won't have built up so much pressure, and it will not likely be that strong. If the first time you experience pīti is in the evening before going to bed, you will probably have trouble getting to sleep. It will wire you up. That's OK. You're learning, and missing a little bit of sleep is worth figuring out how to work with these valuable mental states.

For more scholarly information regarding the sutta description of the first jhāna, see the chapters in Part Two entitled "Vitakka and Vicāra" and "First Jhāna."

Possible Problems Associated with Initially Learning the First Jhāna

Because on account of the presence of pīti there is mental exhilaration, and that state is considered gross. (DN 1.3.23)

The following is not really a problem but bears mentioning: Very often when someone enters the first jhāna, their breath becomes very rough—there are short, sharp gasps that are very unlike the subtle breaths while in access concentration. This is totally normal! Once the pīti and sukha start rising, don't worry in the least what your breathing does—it quite likely will change noticeably. Furthermore, your breathing may not settle back down until you move on toward the second jhāna.

Sometimes, having recently entered the first jhāna for the very first time, one finds that it is much harder to reenter the jhāna. This is usually caused by an increase in wanting—wanting the jhānic experience to reoccur—and the wanting is an instance of the first hindrance, so no jhāna appears. It is important to realize that for most people, when they begin learning the jhānas, they are not going to be experiencing the jhānas every meditation period. Again, the remedy is patience. At first, the mental effort required to generate sufficient concentration and the effort required to patiently wait for the jhāna once the attention has been switched to the pleasant sensation are definitely tiring. It's not uncommon for someone to only be able to generate such effort once a day at first. As one becomes more skilled and more aware of exactly what is needed to generate the jhānas, the mental effort lessens and the jhānas arrive more frequently. Patience and the careful observation of exactly what one has done when the jhāna does appear are the keys to more frequent experiences of jhāna.

The most common problem associated with initially entering the first jhāna is that if it is done late in the evening, it may result in feeling too wired to go to sleep. This usually is a one-time problem most often occurring when someone actually enters the first jhāna for the first time after the evening dhamma talk—that is, right before bedtime. But losing some sleep—even if it's a few hours—is a small price to pay for beginning to gain skill in these very useful states.

Occasionally one successfully enters the first jhāna, but the pīti seems like it's never going to go away. Not only is it not possible to turn down the pīti enough to enter the second jhāna, but the high-energy, buzzing feeling remains even when one gets up from the meditation session. This usually lasts only a few hours or a few days at most. It may generate some insomnia until it calms down; it is definitely an unpleasant condition. It is suggested that if this happens to you, go for a long vigorous walk; do tai chi, yoga, or some other stretching exercises; if possible take a long, hot bath; switch to doing gentle, slow loving-kindness meditation rather than continuing to work with deep concentration. Usually the pīti finally calms down after a good night's sleep—whenever that next happens.

The most serious problem that can arise when attempting to learn the jhānas is fortunately quite rare, occurring in approximately three students per one thousand. This is when the pīti gets stuck on and never seems to go away. This can last for weeks, months, even up to a year. Thankfully this is quite rare since there aren't any really effective solutions other than waiting the thing out. What does seem to help is getting grounded—vigorous exercise, manual labor, and eating heavy foods, like meat (assuming you are not a vegetarian), oils, cheese, and also chocolate.

If you have ever experienced "pīti stuck on," it is important that the next time you do enter the first jhāna, you move quickly toward the second jhāna almost as soon as the pīti begins to build. Don't let the pīti become too strong—take a very deep breath, and let it out completely with total relaxation as you do so; then shift your attention to the sukha, and make that the object of your meditation. Be careful to not let the sukha become too strong! Doing so will pop you back into the first jhāna with its strong pīti. More about this in the next chapter.

5 Second Jhāna

Further, with the subsiding of thinking and examining, one enters and dwells in the second jhāna, which is accompanied by inner tranquility and unification of mind and is without thinking and examining and is filled with rapture and happiness born of concentration. One drenches, steeps, saturates and suffuses one's body with the rapture and happiness born of concentration, so that there is no part of one's entire body not suffused by this rapture and happiness. (DN 2.79)

KEY PALI WORDS:

samādhi	indistractability, concentration
vitakka	thinking
vicāra	examining
pīti	glee, rapture
sukha	happiness/joy

THE THINKING, which was in the background of both access concentration and the first jhāna, subsides when one enters the second jhāna and is replaced by inner tranquility* and unification of mind.† As a practical matter, to move from the first jhāna to the second jhāna, you should take a nice deep breath and let it out slowly and totally, which will calm down the pīti yet leave the sukha strong enough so that you can focus on it. In the first jhāna, the pīti predominates and the sukha is in the background. To move toward the second jhāna, you want to do a foreground-background reversal. When you take the deep breath and deeply exhale, both the pīti and the sukha calm down in intensity, but the pīti drops much more in intensity and is now low-grade and more in the background. The sukha, although perhaps now a bit less intense than it was before the deep breath, is still strong enough to now be the more prominent of the two. The "inner tranquility" mentioned in the description of the second jhāna reflects the shift from an experience of pīti and sukha to an experience of sukha and pīti.

Place your attention on the sukha—that sense of emotional joy/ happiness—and stay focused on it. Its intensity may increase a bit, yet the experience will leave the pīti in the background as long as you don't let the sukha increase too much in intensity. The inner tranquility is a much calmer experience than the experience of the first jhāna. Now let your mind collect on this sense of happiness. In the first jhāna, it is like holding a piece of paper with both hands upon which a marble has been

---

* *Ajjhattaṃ sampasādanaṃ* is often translated as "internal confidence," but in the context of the second jhāna, "inner tranquility" is more accurate as it reflects the calming that takes place in moving from the first jhāna to the second and is in accord with the statement "when one's mind is filled with pīti, one's body becomes tranquil" (which is discussed in chapter 16, "The Jhāna Summary").

† *Ekodi-bhavam,* meaning "concentrated, attentive, fixed" and "become."

placed; you have to really pay attention to hold it steady. But if you let the paper fold up around the marble, then it will stay there easily. This is similar to what is happening here. Your mind collects around the experience of happiness and settles into it, so that it's much less likely to go wandering off. This unification of mind occurs as the thinking subsides and fades away.

You may not experience a level of concentration where the thinking shuts off totally on a retreat of less than a month (or perhaps even longer). Don't worry about that; just get to the point where the sukha predominates and the pīti is in the background. If you can remain fully focused on the sukha, really giving yourself to this experience of happiness/joy, the thinking will indeed subside and fade more and more the longer you stay there without becoming distracted.

In the second jhāna, the pīti is going to be more like rocking or swaying than vibratory in nature—more like what was described as "minor pīti" in the chapter on the first jhāna. The pīti should remain at this minor level as long as you don't let the sukha get too strong. What you want is sukha that is moderately intense and a mind that is strongly unified around this experience of sukha—in other words, moderate happiness/joy, strong one-pointed focus.

In the Poṭṭhapāda Sutta (DN 9.11), we find that after one makes the transition from the first jhāna to the second, "one's former true but subtle perception of pīti and sukha born of seclusion vanishes. At that time there arises a true but subtle perception of pīti and sukha born of concentration, and one becomes one who is conscious of this pīti and sukha." Because the sukha is now in the foreground, it is the object of your attention, but you will be conscious of the minor, background pīti from time to time.

If you find yourself wandering back up toward the first jhāna, in that the pīti is beginning to increase in intensity, take an intentionally deeper breath, and once again bring your attention back to the moderate happiness. In the suttas it says that thinking is a thorn to the second jhāna.[1] So to enhance your experience of the second jhāna, let yourself sink into the quiet stillness of the happiness and just be with it.

Again, the suttas provide a simile:

> Suppose there was a deep lake whose waters welled up from below, it would have no inlet for the water from the East, West, North or South, nor would it be refilled from time to time with showers of rain. And yet a current of cool water welling up from within the lake would drench, steep, saturate and suffuse the whole lake so that there would be no part of that entire lake which is not suffused with the cool water. In the same way, one drenches, steeps, saturates, and suffuses one's body with the rapture and happiness born of concentration, so that there is no part of one's entire body which is not suffused by this rapture and happiness. (DN 2.80)

Notice that in the second jhāna, the rapture and happiness are said to be born of concentration, rather than seclusion. The concentration of the first jhāna has given you the capacity to absorb into the second jhāna via totally giving yourself to the experience of sukha. The simile is of a lake with no streams coming in, no rain, but a spring at the bottom of the lake. This cool water wells up and fills the lake so that there is no part of the lake that is untouched by the cool water. This is an amazingly accurate simile; this is very much what the second jhāna feels like; only it's not cool water—it's happiness that is welling up.

The experience of the second jhāna seems to be located lower in the body than the experience of the first jhāna; it's more in the heart center for most people. It feels like the happiness is coming from your heart and welling up as from a spring. Now, this is not necessarily a steady state.

Many people find that the happiness will tend to increase in intensity for a bit, come down for a bit, and then come back up. It ebbs and flows in a minor way and never fades out. To maintain the second jhāna, just hang out and stay focused on the sense of happiness.

The happiness in this state feels much like ordinary happiness. Imagine it's your birthday and someone gives you a very nice present. You open the present and exclaim, "Wow, this is great! I always wanted one of these," and you are really happy. The happiness of the second jhāna is this kind of happiness, but it isn't triggered by anything external; it's triggered by your concentrated mind. You have a gift within you, and the second jhāna enables you to experience it directly. The sukha initially arose from the concentration generated in access concentration then being focused on pleasure. This brought the first jhāna, consisting of both pīti and sukha, with the pīti predominating. By spending some time in the first jhāna, you stabilized both the pīti and sukha. Now in the second jhāna, you chilled out the pīti and let the sukha dominate your experience. This now ebbing-and-flowing sukha in the second jhāna is a more tranquil experience, and your mind can now absorb into enjoying this sukha. The huge grin of the first jhāna has now likely become a nice big smile.

What you want to do is to be able to get to this state and be able to maintain it for at least 10 to 15 minutes. If you lose it by getting lost in thinking, just come back to the happiness. If you get distracted, the sukha won't entirely disappear at once—there quite possibly will be some weaker remnants of it hanging around when you notice that you've become distracted. Just put your attention on those remnants, and see if the intensity level will come back up to moderate. If not, or if indeed the sukha has completely disappeared, you will need to return to focusing on the breath, mettā, or whatever your access method was, regenerate access concentration, and try again. It is important to give yourself extended time in the second jhāna to let your concentration deepen; the objects of the following jhānas are going to be even more subtle than the sukha of the second jhāna.

For more scholarly information regarding the sutta description of the second jhāna, see the chapter in Part Two entitled "Second Jhāna."

More Possible Problems Associated with Attempting to Learn the Jhānas

To one in the second jhāna, thinking and examining are a thorn. (AN 10.72)

The most common problem encountered when learning the second jhāna results from the fact that the sukha is a more subtle object than the pīti of the first jhāna. It takes a more concentrated mind to be able to stay with this more subtle object. It sometimes happens that you generate strong enough access concentration to be able to enter the first jhāna, but when you move on to the second jhāna, you soon fall out of it. The solution is to stay longer in access concentration and let it deepen before moving to the first jhāna.

Often the distractions that pull you out of the second jhāna arise because the vitakka and vicāra (the thinking) have not really subsided. If you find thinking becoming active in the second jhāna, redouble your efforts to stay completely locked onto the experience of the sukha—give yourself fully to enjoying the happiness/joy. As was mentioned in the previous chapter, on a retreat of less than a month, you are not likely to shut down the thinking entirely in the second jhāna—don't worry about that as long as that thinking is reduced from what you were experiencing in access concentration.

Sometimes what happens when you are trying to learn to enter the first jhāna is that you wind up bypassing the first jhāna unintentionally and end up going directly into the second (or an even higher) jhāna. This is not so unusual and arises when the focus on the pleasant sensation generates strong sukha and weak pīti. Don't worry if this happens to you—just stay focused on the sukha, and enjoy being in the second jhāna. After all, the purpose of the first jhāna is to generate the concentration that will enable you to get to the second jhāna. Usually when this bypassing happens, the vitakka and vicāra (the thinking) has not really subsided—just let your mind gather itself on the experience of sukha so that the thinking does start subsiding more and more.

It's somewhat like starting your car in second gear; you can do it, but you aren't really moving very well at first. So if you bypass the strong pīti experience and wind up having an experience of primarily sukha, just be patient and increase your unification of mind by staying completely focused on the sukha.

Sometimes, however, the access concentration level generated is very strong, and someone bypasses the first jhāna due to this strong initial concentration. That's like starting your car in second gear on a downhill slope—the strong access concentration providing the "downhill"—and the second jhāna initially is quite satisfactory.

If you unintentionally wind up in the second jhāna, stay in it for 10 to 15 minutes to let it grow deeper; then move on to the third jhāna. If this bypassing of the first jhāna keeps happening, stay in the second jhāna for about 5 minutes; then start cranking up the intensity level of the happiness, and see if that pops you "up" into the first jhāna with strong pīti and background sukha. This will give you a direct experience of your "target," and perhaps you can go now from access concentration to the first jhāna.

The reason for learning to go to the first jhāna even if you have good success going directly to the second jhāna is that often entering directly into the second occurs on a retreat when your concentration is exceptional. Your concentration won't be as good when you return home; there, it may be sufficient to enter the first jhāna but not strong enough to go directly into the second. So it's good to know how to get into the jhānas with less concentration, and that usually means knowing how to enter at the first jhāna rather than at the second.

After experiencing both the first and second jhānas, some students want to bypass the first jhāna intentionally because it's too intense. If you want to do this and have sufficient concentration, that's fine. But as mentioned above, if you are doing this on a retreat, your concentration is quite likely to be less when you return home, and going directly to the second jhāna may be far more difficult. It's actually much more useful if you can enter the first jhāna very briefly (a few seconds—maybe even less) and then drop immediately into the second. This is best done by shutting down the pīti as soon as it starts to grow and switching your attention to the sukha. I'd suggest playing with doing the quick-foreground-pīti/drop-to-foreground-sukha-background-pīti and see if that prevents the overly intense pīti.

Very occasionally, after experiencing both the first and second jhānas, some students want to bypass the first jhāna intentionally because the intense pīti brings up painful memories. If this is happening to you, by all means skip the first jhāna. Negative mind states are always counterproductive when trying to generate concentration. Be kind to yourself.

6 Third Jhāna

Further, with the fading away of rapture, one dwells in equanimity, mindful and clearly comprehending, and experiences happiness with the body. Thus one enters and dwells in the third jhāna, of which the noble ones declare: "One dwells happily with equanimity and mindfulness." One drenches, steeps, saturates, and suffuses one's body with happiness free from rapture, so that there is no part of one's entire body that is not suffused by this happiness. (DN 2.81)

KEY PALI WORDS:

samādhi indistractability, concentration
pīti glee, rapture
sukha happiness/joy

THE KEY THING that happens when you enter the third jhāna is that the pīti—the rapture—fades away. You are in a place where you are just happy. But, you are also in a state of equanimity, mindful and clearly comprehending. The best word to describe this state is *contentment.* You are in a state of wishlessness, a state of satisfaction, and you want for nothing. This state is without pīti, so there is no sense of movement. You are very still and happy and hanging out in an ongoing state of wishlessness.

As a practical matter, to get from the second jhāna to the third jhāna, again take a deep breath and let it all out. As you do, dial down the intensity level of the happiness. You're in a bubbly, happy state in the second jhāna; to move to the third, you let that happiness become less intense and begin to fade. As it starts to fade, it might be helpful to remember a time when you were very contented. As an example, you might remember a time when you'd just eaten the perfect meal, you didn't overeat, and you don't have to wash the dishes. Remember the incident briefly—a quarter of a second—and pluck the feeling of contentment out of it. As the happiness of the second jhāna continues to decrease in intensity, put your attention on that feeling of contentment, let the decreasing happiness become that contentment, and let the contentment become the focus of your attention.

At this point, there should be no pīti left at all. The third jhāna is a very still state. There is no sense of movement and the feeling of contentment is rock steady. It usually is not necessary to do anything directly to make the pīti vanish; it seems to fade away on its own as your mental system calms down from happiness to contentment. If there are remnants of pīti left, you didn't quite make it to the third jhāna; you're just in a quieter second jhāna. If this is the case, it's probably good to bring the intensity of the contentment back up to happiness, reestablish your "normal" second jhāna with its foreground sukha and background pīti, and then try again to move to the third jhāna.

The third jhāna is less energetic and feels lower in the body, more toward the belly level. In fact, there is a strong sense of the locus of each jhāna moving physically downward as you go up in the numbers. When someone tells me they went down to the next jhāna, I have to ask if they went down in number from, say, second to first or down in feeling from second to third. The physical sense of descending is so strong that it overrides the idea of going up in number.

Again we have a simile:

> Suppose in a lotus pond there are blue, white or red lotuses that have been born in the water, grow in the water and never rise up above the water, but flourish immersed in the water. From their tips to their roots they would be drenched, steeped, saturated and suffused with water so there would be no part of those lotuses that is not suffused with water. In the same way, one drenches, steeps, saturates and suffuses one's body with the happiness free from rapture so there is no part of one's body which is not suffused by this happiness. (DN 2.82)

The simile is of lotus blossoms that grow up out of the mud but do not come above the surface of the water. They live their entire lives immersed in the water, completely saturated with water. This is a very still picture. The lotuses are not waving around in the breeze; they are not moving with ripples on the pond—there is no movement at all. This is an accurate description of the third jhāna—you are immersed in a sense of contentment with no sense of movement. Being underwater also points to a sense of isolation, which is now beginning to appear as your mind grows even more concentrated.

Once again in the third jhāna, as with the first and the second, the idea is to become so skilled that the sukha—the contentment, which is what the sukha feels like now—seems all-pervasive. And again, don't worry about this when you are first learning the third jhāna. Just get stabilized on the feeling of contentment and hang out while focused on it. Then, when you gain skill at that, you'll find it's not difficult to move it so that it permeates your whole body.

Because the pīti has faded out, this state is a much nicer place to spend time. The sukha still has its nuance of happiness, and that happiness is felt throughout your whole being. The equanimity mentioned in the description of the third jhāna is felt as an unruffled quietness. You don't want anything, nothing is disturbing you, and you sit there with a faint Buddha-like smile on your face. To become skilled in this state, you should learn to maintain it for at least 10 to 15 minutes.

In the Poṭṭhapāda Sutta (DN 9.12), we find that after one makes the transition from the second jhāna to the third, "one's former true but subtle sense of pīti and sukha born of concentration vanishes, and there arises at that time a true but subtle sense of equanimity and happiness, and one becomes one who is conscious of this true but subtle sense of equanimity and happiness." Now the object of attention is the "equanimity and happiness," which can be described best with the word *contentment.*

It is very good to practice moving among the jhānas by going both forward and backward. Once you have learned the third jhāna, try going back "up" to the second jhāna—it will feel like it is physically up, even though the number goes down. The method for doing this is to let the contentment become really, really content—add some excitement to the feeling. This should pop you back up into the second jhāna. You also can go back "up" from the second jhāna to the first. Just let the happiness get more and more happy, even giddily happy—that should bring back up the strong pīti, and you'll find yourself back in the first jhāna. Once you have mastered going both up and down, try moving through the jhānas like 1-2-3-2-3-2-1. Entering a jhāna from both "above" and "below" gives you a clearer picture of exactly what are the qualities of the jhāna, which then enables you to settle more deeply into it.

For more scholarly information regarding the sutta description of the third jhāna, see the chapter in Part Two entitled "Third Jhāna."

Possible Problems Associated with Learning the Third Jhāna

Rapture is a thorn to the third jhāna. (AN 10.72)

The most common problem in trying to learn the third jhāna is that the pīti won't fade away. Rather than entering the third jhāna, you're still in the second but with the sukha intensity turned down. It can never be the third jhāna as long as the pīti remains.

As mentioned in the previous section, the first strategy to try is to return to a more normal second jhāna, hang out there for a few minutes, and then try again to enter the third jhāna. If this doesn't work, sometimes it is helpful to return briefly to the second jhāna and briefly to the first jhāna. As soon as the pīti of the first jhāna is well established, try making it as strong as you can for only a second or two, and then take the deep breath and move toward the second jhāna. Hang out there until the background thinking quiets again; then once more try to enter the third jhāna.

If none of the above work, the next time you move from access concentration to the first jhāna, quickly take the deep breath and move on toward the second jhāna without letting the pīti get so strong. Spend an extra amount of time in the second jhāna before attempting the third again.

Of course if you are dealing with pīti that remains even after you get up from meditating, you are not likely to get it to shut down when you want to go from the second jhāna to the third. In this case you are just going to have to wait out the pīti until it disappears when you are not meditating. Then when you resume your jhāna practice, only stay in the first jhāna a very brief time before taking the deep breath and moving toward the second jhāna.

Another common problem is that the pīti returns after you have been settled in the third jhāna. In that case just ride the experience back up to the second jhāna, stabilize it and hang out in the second jhāna for a few minutes, and then reenter the third jhāna.

7 Fourth Jhāna

Further, with the abandoning of pleasure and pain, and with the previous passing away of joy and grief, one enters and dwells in the fourth jhāna, which is neither pleasant nor painful and contains mindfulness fully purified by equanimity. One sits suffusing one's body with a pure bright mind, so that there is no part of one's entire body not suffused by a pure bright mind. (DN 2.83)

KEY PALI WORDS:

samādhi	indistractability, concentration
adukkha and asukha	neither painful nor pleasant, neither unhappiness nor happiness
somanassa and domanassa	joy and grief
sati	mindfulness
upekkha	equanimity

IN THE THIRD JHĀNA, the focus is on a sense of contentment, and contentment is a pleasant mind state. To move to the fourth jhāna, you want to let go of that pleasure and let your mind go to neutral. When it says, "The abandoning of pleasure and pain and the passing away of joy and grief," it should not be thought that there was pain or grief in any of the previous jhānas. There was certainly pleasure in the first three and joy in the first two. These need to be gone, but not replaced by pain or grief. The aim here is to attain an emotionally neutral state such that your equanimity can fully purify your mindfulness.

As a practical matter, to enter the fourth jhāna, let go of the pleasure of the third jhāna, and hopefully when you do so, there will be a sense of things starting to physically drop down. Go with this sense of dropping down, and continue to let it drop. In the third jhāna, you may find you have a faint smile, a Buddha-like smile. If so, all you have to do is relax the muscles of your face. Both the smile and the sense of pleasure disappear; then usually a sense of things starting to drop down follows. Just stay focused on that sense of dropping, which can continue for quite some time. Eventually the mind settles into a place of quiet stillness. The words in the sutta description are "neither pleasant nor painful" and "equanimity," but it may not be clear what it means to focus on this. A feeling of *quiet stillness* is the best way to describe the experience of the fourth jhāna, and that sense of quiet stillness now becomes the focus. These words simply mean that the fourth jhāna is an emotionally neutral state. There is no pleasure and no pain, only the quiet stillness. The fourth jhāna requires a bit more letting go than any of the previous ones, so let go of anything you are holding on to—that is, fully give yourself to the experience.

Ayya Khema said that being in the third jhāna is like sitting in the mouth of a well—you are a little bit isolated from the world around you. To enter the fourth jhāna, drop down the well to the bottom.[1] Since the fourth requires more letting go than the previous jhānas, don't think of climbing down the well; just let go and drop. The sense of dropping down isn't like a free fall; it's more like drifting down, perhaps like drifting down to the bottom of a swimming pool—another possibly helpful image: in the third you are just under the water; in the fourth you drift down to the bottom. Or in the third you are sitting in the mouth of a cave, and in the fourth you go deep inside the mountain (and the cave has a downward sloping floor).

The feeling of dropping down is so pervasive that you might find yourself physically slumping over. This is a quite common experience and nothing to worry about. As you move from the third jhāna into the fourth, just let go into the feeling of dropping down, and if your body also droops over, let it go into that slump as well. It's true that being in such an awkward posture for an extended period of time is not a physically healthy thing to do, but don't worry about it when you are first learning the fourth jhāna.

When you feel like you are able to establish the fourth jhāna on a regular basis, then you can start working on slumping less. The trick is to allow yourself to slump as you start your "descent" toward the fourth. Then when the slumping gets pronounced, pull yourself physically more upright. This will lessen your concentration a bit and temporarily pause your descent into the depths of the fourth jhāna, but immediately let go again into the sense of dropping down—and let the slumping resume. By repeating this process, you should be able to get all the way down deeply into the fourth jhāna and wind up merely slouching rather than slumping.

In the Poṭṭhapāda Sutta (DN 9.13), we find that, after one makes the transition from the third jhāna to the fourth, "one's former true but subtle sense of equanimity and happiness vanishes, and there arises a true but subtle sense of neither pleasure nor pain, and one becomes one who is conscious of this true but subtle sense of neither pleasure nor pain." Now the object of attention is the even-mindedness of neither pleasure nor pain, but since that is difficult to direct your attention to, direct it to the sense of quiet stillness, and you will automatically be focused on "neither pleasure nor pain."

To be skilled in this state, again you should be able to maintain it for at least 10 to 15 minutes like you did for jhānas two and three. When the fourth jhāna is done well, it is an incredibly restful state. We spend our days thinking and doing and our nights either dreaming or oblivious. Finally now you are in a state where you are fully conscious and almost nothing is happening. Upon emerging from a deep fourth jhāna, you might feel refreshed as though you'd just taken a short nap—but you will be quite certain that you were not asleep. This is a valuable place in and of itself to spend time, given the hectic nature of twenty-first-century civilization.

Once again we have a simile:

> Suppose a man were to be sitting covered from the head down by a white cloth so there would be no part of his entire body not suffused by the white cloth. In the same way, one sits suffusing one's body with the pure, bright mind so that there is no part of one's entire body that is not suffused by a pure, bright mind. (DN 2.84)

The simile is of a man sitting with a white sheet over his head, completely covering him. He's a little isolated from the world around him. The deeper the level of concentration that you bring to the fourth jhāna, the more the sense of isolation and withdrawal from the world around you. It may happen that sounds seem farther away as you get deeper into these states. If your concentration is exceptionally strong, sounds may disappear altogether.

If your concentration level is not exceptionally strong, the reason the simile mentions a "white cloth" and the description uses the word "bright" may not be clear. However, if you spend far more than the 5 to 10 to 15 minutes in access concentration recommended in the chapter "Entering the Jhānas," the diffused white light mentioned in the chapter

"Access Concentration" will become quite steady and strong. After spending an hour or two or three in access concentration, if you then enter the jhānas and work your way down to the fourth one, you will find that your visual field is filled with a bright whiteness, just as if you were sitting in an open field on a sunny day, covered from head to toe with a white sheet and you had your eyes open. At that level of concentration, the simile makes perfect sense.

Understanding this simile also points to the level of concentration that the Buddha and his monastics were working with—and that level of concentration is far more than you are likely to generate in a ten-day retreat. At the time of the Buddha, after the monks and nuns finished their alms rounds, they would eat their midday meal, which would be at around ten or eleven o'clock in the morning. Then they would "go for the day's abiding"[2] and meditate until evening. They probably were not doing 45 minutes of sitting, 45 minutes of walking. These were people who had not grown up with chairs and thus had the capacity to sit cross-legged for an extended period of time. So if they were sitting for multiple hours at a time, over a six- or seven-hour period, they were far more likely to experience a very deep level of concentration. By the time they entered the fourth jhāna, their concentration was deep enough that the simile with its white cloth captures the pure, bright mind they were experiencing.

Unless you are on a retreat of a month or more and are willing to spend an hour or more in access concentration before entering the first jhāna, it will be difficult to reach that level of concentration. But even at a lesser level of concentration, the jhānas are very useful. So don't worry if your visual field is dark rather than white. If you can remain focused on quiet stillness with an equanimous mind, you will generate deep enough concentration to have a strongly enhancing effect on your subsequent insight practice.

For more information about generating the depth of concentration necessary for experiencing the bright white visual field and the strikingly pure, bright mind, see the last question in appendix 1, "Frequently Asked Questions."

Notice also that now "one sits suffusing one's body" rather than "one drenches, steeps, saturates, and suffuses one's body." Clearly things have calmed down quite a lot in the fourth jhāna. Once again in the fourth jhāna, as in the previous jhānas, the idea is to become so skilled that the quiet stillness seems all-pervasive. And again, don't worry about this when you are first learning the fourth jhāna. Just learn to stabilize your attention on the feeling of quiet stillness for ten to fifteen minutes. Then, when you have become skilled at that, you'll find it becomes all encompassing simply by directing your attention throughout your body.

It's also going to be helpful to move up and down through the jhānas: 1-2-3-4-3-2-1 or even 1-2-3-2-3-4-3-4-3-2-3-2-1. Most people find going back "up" to the third jhāna quite easy—just remember what contentment feels like, and make that the object of your attention, adding in a dash of pleasantness. This should pop you back up to the third jhāna. As you go "up" to a lower-numbered jhāna, that lower-numbered one should be stronger than before because you are more concentrated due to having been "down" in the higher-numbered jhāna. If this increased strength is not immediately noticeable, just be patient and let the jhāna experience deepen. The one exception is the first jhāna—the pīti will usually be far less strong than when you initially entered the first jhāna. This is actually a good thing—especially since the strength of a jhāna is not measured by the strength of the primary quality, but by the strength of your indistractable attention upon the primary quality.

Also after you have become skilled in these jhānas, it is not necessary to spend the 10 to 15 minutes in each one every time. Just make sure that you don't always shortchange the same jhāna(s) (although you might always be spending a very short time in the first jhāna before taking the deep breath to move on toward the second jhāna).

For more scholarly information regarding the sutta description of the fourth jhāna, see the chapter in Part Two entitled "Fourth Jhāna."

Possible Problems Associated with Learning the Fourth Jhāna

In-and-out breathing is a thorn to the fourth jhāna. (AN 10.72)

The quiet, still, neutral state of mind that is the object of the fourth jhāna is considerably more subtle than the objects of the previous jhānas. This makes it more difficult to maintain your attention on it. If you find that you are frequently becoming distracted from the fourth jhāna experience or if the background thinking begins to kick in again, it's a sure sign that your concentration level is not strong enough. The best remedy, and the only real long-term solution, is that the next time you are in access concentration, stay longer in access concentration before entering the first jhāna. It is possible to enter the first three jhānas having generated sufficient concentration while in access, but not having generated sufficient concentration to stabilize the fourth jhāna. Counteract this by staying longer in access concentration.

A possible short-term, in-the-moment solution to an unsteady fourth jhāna is to go back "up" to the third jhāna. Hopefully since you are coming from a more deeply concentrated state, you will now experience a deeper third jhāna than before. Stay there for five minutes or more, really giving yourself to the feeling of contentment, and then try again to enter the fourth jhāna. That should give you a more stable experience of the fourth.

Because the fourth jhāna is such a quiet place, your breathing may once again draw your attention—this is of course the thorn being spoken of in the quote above. It is really important if you want a high-quality experience of the fourth jhāna that you ignore your breathing. If you do find your mind wandering to the breathing—which may be less subtle than quiet stillness—you must immediately return your focus to the quiet stillness. If the problem persists, you just don't have sufficient concentration; so try the remedies mentioned above.

Another possible difficulty encountered in the fourth jhāna is that it is such a restful place. If your energy level is not high enough to match your now quite deep concentration, you are likely to fall asleep in the fourth jhāna. If this happens, when you wake up, it probably is going to be a better use of your time to immediately switch to doing an insight practice rather than persisting with doing something you don't have the energy for. It may even be necessary to apply some of the antidotes to sloth and torpor mentioned on the web page "Abandoning the Five Hindrances" at http://rc.leighb.com/more/Abandoning_the_Five_Hindrances.htm.

8 Insight Practice

When one's mind is thus concentrated, pure and bright, unblemished, free from defects, malleable, wieldy, steady and attained to imperturbability, one directs and inclines it to knowing and seeing. One understands thus, this is my body, having material form, composed of the four primary elements, originating from mother and father, built up out of rice and gruel, impermanent, subject to rubbing and pressing, to dissolution and dispersion, and this is my consciousness, supported by it and bound up with it. (DN 2.83)

THE PURPOSE OF THE JHĀNAS is to generate a mind that is concentrated, pure and bright, unblemished, free from defects, malleable, wieldy, steady, and attained to imperturbability, which you can then direct and incline to knowing and seeing. Knowing and seeing what? Body and mind. The jhānas provide you with a mind that can do insight practice more efficiently; they are a warm-up exercise for investigating your body and your mind. Whatever your insight practice is, whatever method you choose to investigate your body and your mind, it will be more effective with a mind that is concentrated, bright, wieldy, and so forth.

We can define an insight as an "understood experience." If you've never tasted a mango and someone describes a mango to you—it's a yellow-orange fruit with a big seed in the middle, you have to peel it, the inside is yellow and juicy and very sweet—do you have any idea what a mango tastes like? Of course not—you think it's a peach! But if you bite into the mango—if you have the experience of tasting a mango—then you know what it tastes like (although of course you only know that's what a mango tastes like if someone tells you that's a mango). You need both—the understanding and the experience. Understanding without any corresponding experience is useful, but not transformative. Experience without understanding is baffling. We need both to progress on the spiritual path. Insight practices are practices—both on and off the cushion—that aim to give us experiences of the true nature of the world in a context such that we can understand them. A partial list of insight practices can be found at http://rc.leighb.com/more/A_Partial_List_of_Insight_Practices.htm.

Insights might be personal—for example, an understanding of a problem you are trying to resolve, or a psychological understanding of why you respond in a certain way to a particular situation. These insights are indeed helpful. In fact a psychological insight may be critical to clear the way to gain deeper, more transformative insights. But deeply transformative insights are impersonal. They are understood experiences of the impermanent, ultimately unsatisfying, empty nature of the universe.

The method for waking up on the spiritual path is to let go, and in order to let go, you need to become convinced there is nothing worth hanging on to—in fact there is nothing you can hang on to. In order to become convinced, you need to investigate reality with a sharp, concentrated mind to clearly see the impermanent, unsatisfactory, and corelessness characteristics of both yourself and the world around you.

One of the things that is most helpful when investigating the nature of reality is to be able to do so from a less egocentric perspective. Normally we approach the world in terms of "Is this something *I* want, or is this something *I* need to get rid of?" It's all about "me," "my wants," "my fears." But although it does seem from a naïve perspective that the world revolves around "me," it's just not so. Practicing the jhānas, with their focus on a series of increasingly subtle objects, quiets down the normal ego-making processes. When you emerge from the jhānas, the ego making does not immediately spring back full-blown—you have some period of time to investigate the world from a much less egocentric perspective. That gives you a far better chance to see what is actually happening instead of seeing the world in terms of your advantages and disadvantages.

This newly generated, less egocentric viewpoint with its pure, bright, malleable, wieldy mind is a temporary experience, and your mind will soon return to its usual egocentric wants and worries. The amount of time this new, more useful viewpoint is available to you is dependent on how much concentration you generated in the jhānas and what you do upon emerging from the jhānas. The very best thing possible to do is to continue your sitting meditation, but now switch to doing some insight practice, some practice of investigating reality. The Buddha recommends that practice be something that helps you understand the characteristics of your body and mind, to see their interdependent relationship and their impermanent nature. For example, the practices given in the Satipaṭṭhāna Sutta, the four establishments of mindfulness, are one establishment of body, three establishments of mind—exactly what is to be investigated with your concentrated mind.

Waking up is a difficult task. It's probably more difficult than cutting a wooden table in two with a dull butter knife. If you really wanted to cut a table in two with a butter knife, you could probably do it. If you pressed really hard, you could make a little dent in it right away. If you kept working and pressing, you could cut that table in two with that dull butter knife. But it would be really hard work and would take a very long time. However, if you were to get a whetstone and put an edge on that butter knife, sharpening it up, then you could cut a lot faster. You would quickly make up all the time you "wasted" putting an edge on the knife.

Of course, after a while the edge would become dull, and you'd have to sharpen it again to keep cutting. Undoubtedly you could cut that table in two a lot faster with a sharp butter knife than with a dull butter knife. The purpose of the jhānas is to sharpen your mind, so that when you look to see what's really happening, you have penetrating insight into it.

In the Tibetan tradition, the bodhisattva of wisdom is Mañjuśrī. Mañjuśrī is often depicted with a sword of wisdom in his right hand, which he uses to cut the bonds of ignorance. Jhāna practice is simply sharpening Mañjuśrī's sword.* By moving though the jhānas, you are making your mind sharp. You haven't cut any bonds of ignorance yet; you still have to wield the sword—that's your insight practice. But if you spend all your time sharpening your sword and never wield it, you never cut any bonds of ignorance—and eventually you'll have no sword left because you would have sharpened it into oblivion.

The transition from the jhānas to insight practice is extremely simple. Stop focusing on the object of the jhāna—for example, the quiet stillness of the fourth jhāna—and start doing your insight practice, whatever it is. You don't have to go backward to the first jhāna and then to access concentration in order to begin. In fact it works best if you begin doing your insight practice from the highest jhāna you know—that's when your concentration is strongest. The sense of the jhāna will remain for at least a few moments, if not longer, when you begin your insight practice, but it will fade away as you continue your insight practice. That's perfectly OK. The jhāna has done its job and gotten you strongly concentrated; let it go, and use your concentrated mind to investigate reality.

It is very helpful when you first sit down to begin your meditation practice to decide what insight practice you will undertake after you

* The metaphor of the sword of wisdom can be traced back to the Pali canon—it appears for example in Dhp 40.

emerge from the jhānas. That way you don't waste any time thinking, "Now what should I do?"—you know what to do with your concentrated, sharp mind. If upon emerging from the jhānas, you really want to do some other practice than the one you decided upon at the beginning of your sitting, it is OK to change your mind once. But whatever insight practice you begin, do continue that insight practice until the end of that meditation period.

What the Buddha discovered was that just doing jhāna practice wasn't sufficient. That's what his first two teachers were teaching him; he left them because concentration practice alone wasn't answering his deep spiritual questions. His genius was in discovering the mind-sharpening capabilities of the jhānas and then knowing how to wield that sharp mind to uncover dependent origination, formulate it in terms of the four noble truths, and then teach it to the rest of us. The jhānas are a warm-up exercise for your insight practice.

For more information regarding the sutta description of insight practice, see the chapter in Part Two entitled "Insight Knowledge" and the web page "A Partial List of Insight Practices" at http://rc.leighb.com/more/A_Partial_List_of_Insight_Practices.htm.

The Two Types of Insight Practice

There are two basic categories into which insight practices can be divided: meditations and contemplations.

Meditations

Meditation techniques involve the wordless, or nearly wordless, examination of some sort of sensory input. It is usually easier to stay focused and not become distracted when doing an insight meditation. And it is easy to recognize that you have become distracted: if you notice thinking happening, you can let go of the thinking and come back to the meditation object.

Contemplations

Contemplation techniques involve thinking about a specific topic. The particulars of a topic may come from sensory input (e.g., contemplating the four elements via sight and touch), or the particulars might come from remembering a teaching and pondering the implications of it (e.g., contemplating dependent origination or contemplating the five daily remembrances given in AN 5.57). It is more difficult to recognize a distraction when contemplating than when meditating since obviously not all thinking is a distraction when contemplating. It is helpful when a contemplation has a word, phrase, or sentence that serves as an initial key to beginning that contemplation. When you recognize a distraction, you can rethink the key to get settled in again.

Both of these are ways of using your jhānically concentrated mind to investigate reality. It is beyond the scope of this book to provide more detail than this—fortunately there are many resources available for learning various insight practices. Please see the web page "A Partial List of Insight Practices" at http://rc.leighb.com/more/A_Partial_List_of_Insight_Practices.htm for examples of each type of these insight practices.

The actual definitions of the words *meditation* and *contemplation* are reversed in Buddhism from what they mean in other religious traditions—and in what they mean based on their linguistic derivations. This is an unfortunate result of the words chosen by the first translators of Buddhist texts into English in the nineteenth century.

9 The Immaterial Jhānas

Four things which were perfectly proclaimed by the Lord . . . [include] . . . four formless states. (DN 33 1.11.7)

From reading the suttas, it would appear that the Buddha considered the fourth jhāna sufficient for generating the "higher mind" of concentration deep enough to enhance your insight practice.* But there are also the four immaterial states, which are sometimes mentioned in the suttas as being practiced after the fourth jhāna. This sequence of eight states of concentration led in the later literature to the four immaterial states being referred to as the *arūpa jhānas*—meaning, "immaterial jhānas." The first four jhānas were then referred to as the *rūpa jhānas*—meaning, "material jhānas."

One of the understandings of the phrase "material jhānas" is that these jhānas have qualities that are possible to experience in the material world. There is a simile based on what is found in the *Visuddhimagga* for these four rūpa jhānas:

> You're lost in the desert and you don't have any water. It's a pretty precarious position. You come over a little rise and in

*Not only does the insight step occur after the fourth jhāna in the gradual training, the phrase "gains at will, without trouble or difficulty, the four jhānas that constitute the higher mind" occurs at MN 6.9, MN 53 (passim), MN 108.17, and MN 119.36

> the distance you see what might be palm trees—or it might be a mirage. You head that way and it's not changing. You start encountering people; they have wet hair, they have bundles of wet clothing; it is an oasis! You get really excited: first jhāna. You come to the oasis, it's beautiful, there's a huge pool of cool, clear water. You're so happy: second jhāna. You drink the water, you jump in, cool off, get cleaned up, get out, you are contented: third jhāna. Then you lie down in the shade of a tree and have a rest: fourth jhāna.[1]

This really does capture what it's like to move through these four states with their familiar glee, happiness, contentment, and equanimity.

The next four states—the arūpa jhānas (the immaterial jhānas)—however are quite unlike anything we have ever experienced in this world. They each have an elaborate name rather than just a number, but there is not much detail given about these states or how to enter them. Pretty much the same terse pattern occurs again and again, although the sparse details decrease as the numbers increase. We'll now take a look at these one by one.

> Here by passing entirely beyond bodily sensations, by the disappearance of all sense of resistance and by non-attraction to the perception of diversity, seeing that space is infinite, one reaches and remains in Sphere of Infinite Space. (DN 33.1.11.7)

So the fifth jhāna, the first of the immaterial attainments, is called "the Sphere of Infinite Space." We could say "realm" or "base" or "place of infinite space" or even "the experience of infinite space." Since at the time of the Buddha, they didn't yet have the concept of zero, it is doubtful they had the concept of infinity. So perhaps a more accurate translation of the name of the fifth jhāna would be "the Realm of Limitless Space" or "the Realm of Endless Space" or "the Realm of Boundless Space."

The description starts by saying, "By passing entirely beyond bodily sensations." In the previous jhānas, you are to drench, steep, saturate, and suffuse your body. But now in order to enter the fifth jhāna, you need to pass beyond any awareness of your body. The objects of these immaterial jhānas are quite subtle, and in order to access them, you need to be very concentrated. That concentration has to be so strong that you're not paying any attention to your physical body; you are just experiencing the mental state of the jhāna.

After "passing entirely beyond bodily sensations," the description continues, "By the disappearance of all sense of resistance and by non-attraction to the perception of diversity." The best way to understand this is to examine an explanation of how to enter the fifth jhāna. When you're in the fourth jhāna, you may find yourself slumped over. Your energy is a bit low, and you should probably bring it up a bit by sitting more upright. Then what you need to do is find something that you can expand without limit. What Ayya Khema taught was to get in touch with the boundaries of your being and expand them so you fill the whole room. Once that feels stable, then expand them to fill the whole building. Once that is feeling fairly stable, then expand them to fill the neighborhood. Then expand farther and farther and farther, all the way to the horizon and beyond; just keep on with the expansion. Once you get to the horizon, let go of the perception of diversity, and then there are no more things you are expanding past. You're not expanding past the moon and then Mars and then Jupiter. Forget all that; just simply focus on the sense of limitless expansion. This expansion needs to go smoothly; there has to be no sense of resistance. If you do encounter any resistance, you have to punch through it and keep expanding ever farther, and doing so smoothly. You just stay focused on that sense of outward expansion.

Remember in order to get to the first jhāna,

- you generate access concentration, and
- then after spending some time there,
- you find something pleasant and
- stay focused on that pleasure.

Here you are to

- imagine something you can expand,
- starting out by expanding past the things in your vicinity,
- expand farther past all objects, and
- stay focused on the sense of expansion.

If you can do so, eventually, a vast, empty space will appear before you. Don't look for the space; if you do that, you are not focused on the expansion and thereby prevent the infinite space from appearing. You have to just focus on the expansion, and eventually the endless space will come and find you. The first jhāna was not the pleasant sensation to which you switched your attention—you needed the pīti and sukha. This expansion is not the fifth jhāna—you need to wait patiently for the infinite space to appear.

You can do as Ayya Khema taught and expand the boundaries of your being. But it turns out that it doesn't matter what you expand. A student reported taking an imaginary balloon and blowing it up bigger and bigger and bigger, until it popped and there was the space. She was also the one who took a flashlight and followed the beam of light farther and farther and farther until it illuminated the space. Another student described riding an elevator farther and farther. People have mentioned imagining riding a rocketship farther and farther away or even listening to an actual airplane fly over and then following the sound as it went way off into the distance. It doesn't matter what you are mentally expanding. What matters is that you can keep focused on that sense of expansion.

You don't want to try and expand in all directions—that's too complex. Generally, you want to at most pick two directions you can move your arms in symmetrically: out to the side along the X-axis or maybe up in front of you. Most people like to go up and out. Just stay focused on the sense of expansion.

When the space appears, it's pretty obvious. Your reaction is likely to be something like "Oh wow, that's a big space!" It's as though you're walking along in the Arizona desert and you suddenly come to the Grand Canyon; only this time there is no bottom, and there is no other side. It's a very big space! And it's unmistakable when it appears.

If you are a visual person, you will likely "see" the space. Sometimes it appears as off-white or light gray—there may or may not be a horizon line. Sometimes it appears as black, such as outer space—but with no perception of diversity, there are no stars or galaxies or anything like that; it's just empty black space. If you are not a visual person, you might not "see" the space, but somehow you will know it's there. Whether you "see" it or not, when it appears, let go of your focus on the expansion, put your full attention on the spaciousness of the space, and just sit there experiencing that. In the Poṭṭhapāda Sutta (DN 9.14), we find that after you make the transition from the fourth jhāna to the sphere of infinite space, "one becomes one who is conscious of this true but subtle perception of the Sphere of Infinite Space."* The object of attention is this experience of boundless space.

* This statement is left out of Walshe's translation of Dīgha Nikāya 9, but it does appear in

In this state, there is a very tiny sense of an observer that is observing this vast space before you. You won't really notice the observer the first several times you're in the fifth jhāna. It's only after you have become skilled at it that you realize afterward, "Oh yes, there was a tiny observer and all that huge space before me." When the fifth jhāna becomes really strong, the vast space is not only before you, but below and above and behind and all around, with the observer suspended in the middle. But for most people, when they first start entering the fifth jhāna, the space is only in front of them; it's only with skill and deeper concentration that the space is all encompassing.

As for the previous jhānas, you want to learn to maintain this state for 10 to 15 minutes. So you just sit there focused on the spaciousness that is the fifth jhāna.

> By passing entirely beyond the Sphere of Infinite Space, seeing that consciousness is infinite, one reaches and remains in Sphere of Infinite Consciousness. (DN 33.1.11.7)

The instructions are getting a bit sparse. So, you're sitting there, and you're focused on this vast space. The trick for moving to the sixth jhāna is to shift your attention from the space to your consciousness of the space. Become aware of your awareness; become conscious of your consciousness. It's a trick of turning your attention back on itself. Since you can't be conscious of a limitless space with a limited consciousness, when you turn your attention back to your consciousness, lo and behold, it's as big as the limitless space, and you are now aware of having a limitless consciousness. What it seems like is that initially there is the vast space

the Pali at D 1.183. Thanissaro Bhikkhu translates the full passage at www.accesstoinsight.org/tipitaka/dn/dn.09.0.than.html.

before you, you turn your attention back to your consciousness, you become absorbed into the space, and you become an infinite consciousness. Now the observer and the observed are the same, although again you might not notice this when you are first learning the sixth jhāna. It feels as though your mind got very big, unlimited. Those people who describe it as having any sort of visual appearance usually describe it as dark. That's about it, other than this sense of "my mind is really big." It's an even more subtle state than the realm of infinite space.

In the Poṭṭhapāda Sutta (DN 9.15), we find that after you make the transition from the sphere of infinite space to the sphere of infinite consciousness, "one becomes one who is conscious of this true but subtle perception of the Sphere of Infinite Consciousness."* Now your attention is on the experience of infinite consciousness.

Sometimes when the sixth jhāna is very strong, it can feel as though there are other consciousnesses within this boundless consciousness—some little consciousnesses over here, some other little consciousnesses over there. It's not like you can read the minds of these other little consciousnesses. It's just a feeling, but it only occurs when your concentration is quite strong. If it happens, there is nothing you need to do; you just notice that it seems like there are other consciousnesses within this vast, limitless consciousness. And it's only going to happen if your concentration is exceptionally strong.

If someone comes from a spiritual tradition where the goal of their spiritual practice is union with a higher self, union with *ātman* (Pali: *atta*), and they experience the sixth jhāna, they might think they've done what needed to be done. "There's this infinite consciousness and

---

* Again this statement is left out of Walshe's translation of Dīgha Nikāya 9, but it does appear in the Pali at D 1.184. Thanissaro Bhikkhu translates the full passage at http://www.accesstoinsight.org/tipitaka/dn/dn.09.0.than.html.

it's me; I must now have achieved union with ātman, right?" Wrong, it's just an experience. You have put your brain/nervous system into an altered state, such that what you are experiencing is perceived by you as you having an infinite consciousness—that's all. It's certainly a very concentrated state, but it's not union with any ātman.* Hang out and focus on how big the consciousness is. Then the sense of this being your consciousness is very tiny; what's obvious is that you are focused on a boundless consciousness.

When you are first learning the sixth jhāna, there might not seem to be a whole lot of difference between the fifth jhāna and the sixth. It's a subtle shift unless your concentration is really strong and you are quite familiar with the qualities of both jhānas. It's very helpful to go back and forth a few times between jhānas five and six—1-2-3-4-5-6-5-6-5-6—staying in both five and six for at least five minutes each time to let them deepen. You also want to become skilled enough that you can enter this state of infinite consciousness and remain in it for 10 to 15 minutes before moving on to learning/entering the next jhāna.

> By passing entirely beyond the Sphere of Infinite Consciousness seeing that there is no thing, one reaches and remains in the Sphere of No-Thingness. (DN 33.1.11.7)

Maurice Walshe, in his translation of the Dīgha Nikāya, used "no-thingness," rather than "nothingness," which is a very good idea since it gives a more accurate description of what the jhāna experience is like. It's necessary in moving from the sixth jhāna toward the seventh to conjure up a sense of nothing. The trick is to become aware of the content

* Of course the Buddha's teaching of anatta—"no *ātman*"—denies the existence of any ātman with which to experience union.

of this infinite consciousness. The sense of space is long gone, and you realize the consciousness is not conscious of anything. It is conscious of nothing, *no-thing.* Put your attention on that sense of no-thing. The nothing, at first, may be a small nothing, sort of a basketball-sized nothing in front of your face. Then as you stay with it, you realize there's nothing over here and nothing over there and nothing back there or anywhere. Then the nothing seems to be bigger, although it never really gets that infinite feel that you have in the fifth jhāna of the realm of infinite space, or the sixth jhāna of the realm of infinite consciousness. It just sort of goes from a little nothing to a big nothing to an even bigger nothing.

It's like if you go down into the basement, turn on the light switch, and it doesn't work. You peer into the darkness trying to determine what's in the basement. You can see faintly there is nothing right in front of you. As your eyes get a little more adjusted, you see there is nothing over here and there's nothing over there—why, there is nothing down here at all! It's that kind of nothing.

Look around the room you are currently in—most likely the room has a bunch of stuff in it. Suppose the next time you are gone from this room for an extended time, someone comes in and takes everything away. When you next return, there's nothing here. The seventh jhāna is that kind of nothing.

This no-thingness is not the emptiness that is talked about so often in Mahayana tradition; that's a very different concept—it refers to things being empty of any inherent existence, and recognition of it occurs in more of an insight state than a concentration state. The no-thingness of the seventh jhāna is like you take the lid off the cookie jar and there is nothing in there. It is not the emptiness that is being referred to; it's the fact that there is no thing to perceive. Put your attention on the no-thingness. In the Poṭṭhapāda Sutta (DN 9.16), we find that after you make the transition from the sphere of infinite consciousness to the sphere of no-thingness, "one becomes one who is conscious of this true but subtle perception of the Sphere of No-Thingness."

The no-thingness can manifest visually in two different ways, though of course it doesn't have to manifest visually, especially if you are not a visual person. The most common way it manifests is as blackness or deep purple or dark blue—much like if you were peering into a room with no windows and no lights. There is a sense of space there, but what really gets your attention is not the space but the overwhelming sense that there is nothing at all to be found in that space. In the fifth jhāna, there is *a big space* with nothing in it; in the seventh jhāna, there is *nothing* as far into the space as you can sense.

The best way to get a sense of the other visual way the seventh jhāna can manifest would be to remember how on an old TV if you turned to a channel with no station, you got black-and-white static. Some people see something somewhat like that in the seventh jhāna, only it's black-and-black static.

There is a tiny sense of an observer suspended in the nothing. First, perhaps, there is only nothing in front of you, but as the jhāna gets more refined and you get deeper into it, there is nothing beside you or below you or behind you or above you. The sense of an observer is really tiny, much smaller than in the fifth jhāna, but still on reflection afterward, you know there was a tiny point of observation suspended in the middle of nothing.

Sometimes, people stumble into this state by accident. They're usually on very long retreat and are just meditating away, doing their vipassanā practice, for example, and suddenly they fall into the void. It's pretty terrifying, because to go from ordinary consciousness into the seventh jhāna, you have to be extremely concentrated. With that much concentration, the experience is going to be really intense. I have had students come to an interview and ask, "Can I tell you about something that happened? I was sitting in a long retreat and was just meditating, and I fell into the void." I ask them what happened next, and they usually say, "I went running to the teachers, and they told me to go take a shower, get something to eat, and get calmed down, get grounded." I ask them to describe "the void," and after they do so, I say, "It sounds to me like the seventh jhāna. I'm not sure. I guess we won't really know until you get back there." They usually say, "I don't know if I want to go back there. It was really scary!" But, eventually they learn the first six jhānas and come once more for an interview. I give them the instructions for the seventh jhāna, and they say, "I don't know if I want to go back there." I say, "It'll be fine; just go try it." So they follow the instructions and come back and say, "Yes, yes, that's exactly where I was! Only this time it wasn't scary." The fear that arose was fear of the unknown—they didn't know what was happening to them. But there is nothing frightening about the seventh jhāna in and of itself. There is nothing there, so there is nothing to be frightened of. It's actually a pretty cool place to hang out. There's nothing to disturb you.

Again you want to become skilled enough that you can enter this state and remain in it for 10 to 15 minutes before moving on.

> By passing entirely beyond the Sphere of No-Thingness, one reaches and remains in the Sphere of Neither-Perception-Nor-Non-Perception. (DN 33.1.11.7)

There is not much in the way of instructions or even description of the sphere of neither perception nor nonperception. "Perception" is a translation of the Pali word *saññā*. *Saññā* often refers to your capacity to label things, to identify them, to look them up in your database of objects and give them a name. Look around your current environment, and what do you notice? If you start naming what you notice, that's saññā. Saññā is perception, identifying, naming; so the eighth jhāna is the state of neither identifying nor not identifying, neither naming nor not naming.*

This state is hard to describe because it's a state that has no characteristics that you can use to identify it, other than the fact that it's a state that has no characteristics you can use to identify it. But there is good news. If you have a good, solid seventh jhāna—a good, solid nothing—let it collapse and come to rest in front of your face. Then see if your mind will go into a state that has no characteristics (and yet, you can stay in that state). It's very hard to describe, but it is fairly easy to find if you have sufficient concentration.

The Poṭṭhapāda Sutta (DN 9) does not mention the realm of neither perception nor nonperception, so there is no description of the object of the eighth jhāna. And in fact, it is very difficult to put into words just exactly what the object is—other than the object is the experience that has no characteristics that you can use to identify it. Like the fourth jhāna, it is a very restful state; sometimes it feels almost like you could just lean your head against it and rest, although, of course, there is not anything to lean your head against.

The realm of neither perception nor nonperception is far more subtle than the previous jhānas, and that makes it far more difficult to sustain than previous ones. In each of the jhānas, there is the object of your attention—for example, the contentment in the third jhāna—and your one-pointed attention on that object. The depth of any jhāna is not based on how strong the object is, but rather on how unlikely you

---

* *Saññā* can also mean "consciousness"; hence the eighth jhāna could also be translated as "neither consciousness nor unconsciousness." See chapter 18, "The Immaterial States," for further discussion.

are to become distracted from that object. In any jhāna, it is possible to wobble if your concentration is not strong enough—to be fully with the object for a time and then to begin to slip off into distraction, thinking. If you catch yourself soon enough, you can quickly return to the object of that jhāna and then restabilize the jhāna. The contentment, for example, does not immediately disappear the instant you become distracted; rather it fades out over a period of a few seconds to a few minutes. What is happening is that you are in the jhāna, lose it for a short time, and then regain the jhāna. Of course this wobbling is not nearly as useful as never being distracted from the object of the jhāna, but given the depth of your concentration—or lack thereof—this sort of wobbling might be happening. This wobbling can even happen with the seventh jhāna, although there you have a much shorter time to be "gone" before the sense of nothingness disappears entirely.

However with the eighth jhāna, you might have time for one brief sentence—not containing the words *I, me,* or *mine*—before it completely disappears. It's a very subtle state and disappears quite quickly if you lose your attention on it. This makes it far more fragile than any of the previous jhānas. If you do successfully learn to enter the realm of neither perception nor nonperception and then become distracted and find no trace of the jhāna to return to when you recognize the distraction, it will then be necessary to go back to the seventh or perhaps even to the fifth and work your way back to the eighth jhāna.

Once you have learned all eight jhānas, it is a good idea to practice 1-2-3-4-5-6-5-6-7-6-7-8-7-8-7-6-7-6-5, going back and forth, up and down among the four immaterial jhānas. It is also good to practice 1-2-3-4-5-6-7-8-7-6-5-4-3-2-1. These four immaterial jhānas will deepen your concentration so that you have a mind that is even more concentrated, purer, brighter, more malleable, wieldier, steadier, and more imperturbable. This will enhance your insight practice by enabling you to have an even less egocentric viewpoint and maintain it for an even longer period of time.

For more information about these immaterial jhānas, see the chapter in Part Two entitled "The Immaterial States."

Possible Problems Associated with Learning the Immaterial Jhānas

The most common problem encountered in learning the fifth jhāna is not having strong enough concentration. The transition from the fourth jhāna to the fifth is the most difficult one for most people. You are exiting a state where there is still enough sense of your physical body that you can "sit suffusing [your] body with a pure bright mind," but in order to enter the realm of infinite space, you have to "pass entirely beyond bodily sensations." In order to make the transition, you are going to need a nice, strong experience of the fourth jhāna. As mentioned earlier, if the fourth jhāna is not feeling strongly concentrated, it might be useful to go back to the third jhāna and then return to the fourth after letting the third jhāna deepen for multiple minutes. And of course, the best remedy when encountering concentration that is not strong enough in any situation is to spend more time in access concentration before initially entering the jhānas.

Another very common problem is impatience. You might spend several minutes trying to stay focused on the sense of outward expansion but become tempted to "look for" the infinite space. That won't work—doing so means you are losing your focus on the outward expansion. It really does require that you just sit back, relax, and stay with the expansion. Don't worry; when you do arrive in the fifth jhāna, you will unmistakably recognize it.

Occasionally students report feeling like there is something in front of them that is impeding the expansion. If this occurs, switch to expanding directly into whatever it is that is impeding you, and push it farther and farther away. Sometimes this is all that is necessary to complete the transition to the fifth jhāna; otherwise, when it has been pushed so far away that it no longer feels like it is impeding in any way, you can either resume expanding as before or just continue expanding in the direction you pushed it away.

If the expansion fails to take you into the realm of infinite space after about five minutes, let go of expanding and drop back "down" into the fourth jhāna. Assuming there is still plenty of time left in your meditation session, you can let the fourth deepen and then try once again.

A problem common to all the immaterial jhānas is that all four objects of attention are very subtle. If your concentration is not strong enough, you might indeed be able to enter one of them but not be able to sustain it. If you find your mind wobbling, drop back to the previous jhāna, reestablish it firmly, stay longer in it than you did previously, and then try reentering that jhāna.

Sometimes the shift from the infinite space to your consciousness of the infinite space is difficult to do, or it even may be unclear as to what to do. It's a good idea to become familiar with making this shift with far less subtle objects: stare at some object in your room for ten seconds or so; then see if you can become aware of your awareness of that object. Practice this until the shift is clear, and it can make it much easier to shift from the fifth to the sixth jhāna.

Occasionally when a student is attempting to move from the fifth to the sixth jhāna, they wind up skipping the sixth jhāna and enter the seventh jhāna of no-thingness. This is usually triggered by putting more attention on the fact that the infinite space has nothing in it, rather than putting your attention on your awareness of the space. If this happens, it's good to remain in the seventh jhāna for a few minutes and then drop back into the fifth jhāna. Again it might be necessary to expand something to reestablish the fifth, but it usually is fairly easy to reenter. Then remain for several minutes in the infinite space, and try once again shifting your attention to your consciousness of the space.

Because the realm of neither perception nor nonperception is far more subtle than any of the other jhānas, you are going to need to be quite skilled at the realm of no-thingness in order to find it. It is very important to spend a longer than usual time in the seventh jhāna before trying to move on to the eighth. When you feel like the seventh is very firmly established and are certain you've been in it long enough, stay in a little longer before letting the no-thingness collapse.

Although I stated earlier that you should "begin doing your insight practice from the highest jhāna you know," the eighth jhāna is not all that well suited for doing an insight practice that requires thinking, for example contemplating the five daily remembrances or dependent origination. If you are going to be doing a contemplation for your insight practice and you have attained the eighth jhāna, it might be better to go backward to the seventh jhāna, stabilize it, and then begin your contemplation. But if you are going to be doing an insight practice that is more meditative, such as a body scan or noticing vedanā, the eighth jhāna is a suitable jumping off place.

10 With a Mind Thus Concentrated

Here, bhikkhus, quite secluded from sensual pleasures, secluded from unwholesome states, a bhikkhu enters upon and abides in the first jhāna . . . the second jhāna . . . the third jhāna . . . the fourth jhāna. This is called the bliss of renunciation, the bliss of seclusion, the bliss of peace, the bliss of enlightenment. I say of this kind of pleasure that it should be pursued, that it should be developed, that it should be cultivated, and that it should not be feared. (MN 139.9)

THE JHĀNAS and the immaterial states seem to be naturally occurring states of mind. Approximately 10 percent of the students I've worked with report having experienced one (and sometimes more) jhānas as a child.* Occasionally they tell me this based on my description of the jhānas; more often they report this after learning to enter a jhāna, noticing how familiar the state seems, and then remembering having entered that state as a child.

Far more students report having experienced one or more of these states while on a previous meditation retreat. These are not superhuman mind states—they arise naturally when your mind is sufficiently concentrated and you turn it toward a thought or feeling that is close enough to

*In MN 36.31, the Buddha recounts remembering a childhood experience of the first jhāna.

the experience of a jhāna. In chaos theory there is the notion of an *attractor.* An attractor represents a state into which a system finally settles. If we start with different initial conditions for the system, under certain circumstances, we find the same pattern emerging. The circumstances for which this holds true is called the *basin of attraction* for the attractor. It seems as though the jhānas are attractors; if your mental system gets close enough to one of the attractors—that is, you have sufficient concentration plus some other mental factor(s), such as pleasure or joy or contentment or the notion of vast space—you are in the basin of attraction for that jhāna and settle into the pattern that we call the jhāna.

In ornithology there is the notion of a *search image. Search image* is defined by Luuk Tinbergen[1] as a typical image of a prey that a predator can remember and use to spot prey when that image is common. In a natural foraging situation, a bird's most effective strategy is to maximize its food intake while minimizing energy expenditure.[2] Use of a search image enables a bird of prey to quickly "sort" visual input into that which can be ignored and that which should be pursued. The descriptions of the jhānas given above are search images. Do not take them as absolutes; use them as a generalized description of the states you are seeking when your concentration is excellent. This will maximize your chances of finding these states as they manifest for you while minimizing your mental energy expenditure.

The jhānas were not invented; they were discovered. People in India had been practicing mindfulness of breathing for many centuries by the time of the Buddha. They had been stumbling into deep, stable states of concentration for a very long time. Eventually these states were codified and arranged in order of increasing subtlety of object. By the fifth century B.C.E., these were well known and were being taught—Master Gotama learned them from his two teachers before he became the Buddha.

Although the principle is not mentioned explicitly in the suttas, the depths of these jhānic experiences are dependent on the depth of concentration. It seems there are two ways to increase the depth of the jhānas: stay longer in access concentration and stay longer in the jhānas that precede the jhāna you wish to deepen. Since the meditation objects used in access concentration are less subtle than the objects of the jhānas, it is often more useful to remain in access concentration a longer time if one wishes to experience deep jhānas.

It almost seems like the jhānas are a multiplier—whatever depth of concentration you bring to your initial jhānic experience can be doubled or tripled by moving through the jhānas. For example (using numbers completely pulled out of thin air), suppose moving from the first to fourth jhāna doubles your concentration and moving on to the eighth jhāna doubles that again. Then if you enter the first jhāna with 3 units of concentration, moving to the fourth will give you 6 units and moving on to the eighth will give you 12 units. But if you enter the first jhāna with 20 units of concentration, moving to the fourth yields 40 units and moving on to the eighth yields 80 units of concentration. Remember all these numbers are *bogus;* but hopefully the above gives you a sense of what the jhānas can do for your concentration.

It is also important to remember that the jhānas are not a big deal—they are a useful deal, but people should never laud or disparage themselves because they can or cannot enter a jhāna. In the Sappurisa Sutta (MN 113.21), the Buddha says:

> But a true man considers thus: "Non-identification even with the attainment of the first jhāna has been declared by the Blessed One; for in whatever way they conceive, the fact is ever other than that." So, putting non-identification first, he neither lauds

> himself nor disparages others because of his attainment of the first jhāna. This too is the character of a true man.

The Buddha then goes on to repeat this for all eight jhānas. The jhānas are useful for people who can enter them and use them wisely. But people have all sorts of talents. Some people have talents that make jhāna practice doable, and others have different talents. Basically if you do have talents that enable you to learn the jhānas, then you should use those talents on the spiritual path. If you don't have those talents, use the ones you have.

At times I have been accused of teaching "Jhāna Lite." It's certainly true that what I am teaching is "lite" compared to what is described in the *Visuddhimagga,* but as you'll see in Part Two of this book, what is described in the *Visuddhimagga* doesn't match what is described in the suttas. Certainly the experience of students first learning the jhānas on a ten-day meditation course is going to be lighter than what is possible on a longer retreat after they have developed skill in these states. And what students initially learn on a ten-day retreat is going to be "lite" compared to what is described in the suttas. But there are three very important advantages to learning these so-called lite jhānas:

- They can be learned by a significant percentage of people who have a good daily meditation practice at the time they begin the attempt to learn them.
- The jhānas learned on a ten-day meditation retreat can be used very fruitfully to enhance insight practice to a remarkable degree.
- By staying longer in access concentration, the depth of these so-called lite jhānas can be strengthened so that they do closely match the descriptions given in the suttas.

The Buddha was one of the most practical people who ever lived. He wasn't interested in answering metaphysical questions, such as how the world began. He just wanted people to practice as best they could, given their life circumstances, so that they could reduce or even eliminate their dukkha. From a practical standpoint, it is far better to engage in a practice you can actually do than to hold out trying to learn some practice that is beyond your capacity given your current circumstances. Since most people reading this book are not living a lifestyle that is conducive to generating on a daily basis the really deep concentration that can arise on a retreat of a month or longer, it seems to be much better to teach in a way that allows a student to work with the concentration that is available to them and use that to enhance their practice. Even if the jhānas you learn are "Jhāna Lite," they have the capacity to recharge your meditation practice; they provide a very wholesome source of pleasure—something the Buddha felt was necessary on the spiritual path; and they can enhance your insight meditation practice strongly enough so that you gain life-changing insights.

PART TWO

Demystified Jhānas

Introduction to Part Two

THE DESCRIPTION OF THE JHĀNAS presented in Part One of this book is not an orthodox understanding of the jhānas. The orthodox Theravadan understanding of jhānas is based on the *Visuddhimagga,* which was written more than eight centuries after the death of the Buddha and describes extremely deep states of concentration. The orthodox Tibetan understanding of jhānas also describes states of extremely deep concentration. It is highly unlikely the Tibetan view was derived from the Theravadan view or vice versa. It is far more likely both understandings were derived from a common source that existed in ancient India before the saṅgha divided into the various Sthaviravāda and Mahayana sects, the latter of which later spread to Tibet. Both schools claim that common source was the Buddha. I'm claiming otherwise.

As I learned from Ajahn Buddhadasa, if you are going to write something that is different from what the orthodox teachings are, you better back it up with impeccable sutta scholarship. So this second part of the book is that sutta scholarship. It contains a detailed examination of what can be found in the suttas regarding the jhānas. This examination shows that the orthodox views of the jhānas conflict with what the suttas actually describe and, furthermore, shows that the practices described in Part One are in accord with the suttas.

11 Vitakka and Vicāra

One enters and dwells in the first jhāna, which is accompanied by vitakka and vicāra. (DN 2.77)

KEY PALI WORDS:

vitakka thinking
vicāra examining

PERHAPS NO ASPECT OF THE FIRST JHĀNA as described in the suttas is more misunderstood than the words *vitakka* and *vicāra*. They are often translated as something like "initial and sustained thinking" or "initial and sustained application" or "initial and sustained attention on the meditation object." It is true that this is the meaning of these words in later Buddhism, particularly in the commentaries, but this is definitely not the meaning in the suttas—ever. At the time of the Buddha and probably for more than a century after his death, *vitakka* meant "thinking," and *vicāra* meant "examining" or "pondering" or "evaluating" or "considering."

The combination "vitakka and vicāra" is a case of *synonymous parallelism,* a rhetorical device, which occurs very frequently in the suttas. Just like the phrase "One drenches, steeps, saturates, and suffuses one's body with this rapture and happiness" does not indicate four different things to do, the phrase "vitakka and vicāra" does not indicate two different qualities/factors/aspects. The use of "vitakka and vicāra" is just stressing that thinking is indeed happening in the first jhāna and totally goes away in the second jhāna.[1]

There is a very interesting note under the definition of *vitakka* in the Pali Text Society's dictionary:

> Looking at the combination vitakka+vicāra in earlier and later works one comes to the conclusion that they were once used to denote one & the same thing: just thought, thinking, only in an emphatic way (as they are also semantically synonymous), and that one has to take them as one expression, . . . without being able to state their difference. With the advance in the Saṅgha of intensive study of terminology they became distinguished mutually. Vitakka became the inception of mind, or attending, and was no longer applied, as in the Suttas, to thinking in general.

Footnote 611 in Maurice Walshe's translation of the Dīgha Nikāya reads:

> Vitakka-vicāra. . . . I have used the rendering mentioned at n.80 ['thinking and pondering'], instead of the more usual 'initial and sustained application'. In a private communication, L. S. Cousins writes: 'The words simply do not mean this . . . Suttanta does not distinguish between access and absorption—hence the terms used do not have their momentary Abhidhamma sense. In the case of vicāra this is not even the Abhidhamma sense, since the Dhammasaṅgaṇī* clearly explains vicāra as "investigating".'

* The *Dhammasaṅgaṇī* (Enumeration of phenomena) is one of the books of the Pali Abhidhamma. However, in its description of the first jhāna, *vicāra* does seem to imply "sustained attention" since ekaggata (one-pointedness) has been added as a factor of the first jhāna.

Vitakka is a much more commonly occurring word in the suttas than *vicāra*—in fact, in the PTS *Pali-English Dictionary* by T. W. Rhys Davids under *vicāra* we find:

> Hardly ever by itself (as at Th 1, 1117 manovicāra), usually in close connection or direct combination with vitakka.

Footnote 436 in Bhikkhu Bodhi's translation of the numerical discourses mentions that "vicāra originally meant 'traveling around.'"[2] This certainly gives much more of a sense of "examining" or "pondering" or "turning over in the mind" and really seems to be the opposite of "sustained attention."

Vitakka occurs in the titles of a pair of suttas:

- Majjhima Nikāya 19—Dvedhāvitakka Sutta
- Majjhima Nikāya 20—Vitakkasaṇṭhāna Sutta

and these are very definitely all about thinking and contain nothing about initial application or initial attention.

In the Saṃyutta Nikāya at SN 21.1, Mahāmoggallāna reports about when he was first learning the jhānas and wondered:

> "What now is noble silence?"
>
> Then, friends, it occurred to me: "Here, with the subsiding of thinking and examining, a bhikkhu enters and dwells in the second jhāna, which has inner tranquility and unification of mind, is without thinking and examining, and has rapture and happiness born of concentration. This is called noble silence."

See the web page "Abhidhamma Jhānas" at http://rc.leighb.com/more/Abhidhamma_Jhanas.htm for more information.

In SN 41.6, Citta (the householder) asks Venerable Kāmabhū, "What is the verbal formation?" He is told, "Thinking and examining are the verbal formation." Citta then asks, "Why are thinking and examining the verbal formation?" He is told, "First one thinks and examines, then afterwards one breaks into speech; that is why thinking and examining are the verbal formation."

These two suttas clearly show that *vitakka* and *vicāra* do indeed refer to thinking. And since the first one at SN 21.1 is in reference to the second jhāna, there is no way *vitakka* and *vicāra* can mean anything like "initial and sustained attention/application" in the context of the jhānas in the suttas.

In the Saṃyutta Nikāya at SN 40.2, we find a passage that is parallel to what occurs in SN 21.1, mentioned above, and again Mahāmoggallāna reports about when he was first learning the jhānas:

> "Then, friends, with the subsiding of thinking and examining, I entered and dwelt in the second jhāna. . . . While I dwelt therein perception and attention accompanied by thinking and examining assailed me.
>
> "Then, friends, the Blessed One came to me by means of spiritual power and said this: 'Moggallāna, Moggallāna, do not be negligent, brahmin, regarding the second jhāna. Steady your mind in the second jhāna, unify your mind in the second jhāna, concentrate your mind in the second jhāna.' Then, on a later occasion, with the subsiding of thinking and examining, I entered and dwelt in the second jhāna, which has inner tranquility and unification of mind, is without thought and examination, and has rapture and happiness born of concentration."

Here we see thinking—vitakka and vicāra—arising to disturb Mahāmoggallāna's second jhāna.

Now, it's true that quite likely the whole Moggallāna Saṃyutta (SN 40) is a late composition since "virtually the entire Moggallāna Saṃyutta" is missing from the Chinese āgamas,[3] but this just further points to the fact that for a very long time after the death of the Buddha, *vitakka* and *vicāra* never meant anything like "initial and sustained application" or "initial and sustained attention on the meditation object."

In fact, even the translation of *vitakka* and *vicāra* as "thinking and examining" does not really accurately capture the meaning the phrase "vitakka and vicāra" has in relation to the jhānas. Remember above, Rhys Davids indicates that in the suttas, they are "used to denote one & the same thing: just thought, thinking, only in an emphatic way." Perhaps the best translation of the sutta description of the first jhāna would be

> Quite secluded from sense pleasures, secluded from unwholesome states, one enters and dwells in the first jhāna, which is accompanied by *thinking and more thinking* and filled with the rapture and happiness born of seclusion. (DN 2.77; emphasis mine)

Equally the sutta description of the second jhāna is actually emphasizing, by mentioning it twice, that the thinking that occurred in the first jhāna has ceased; the description could more accurately be translated as

> Further, with the subsiding of *all thinking,* one enters and dwells in the second jhāna, which is accompanied by inner tranquility and unification of mind and is without *any thinking* and is filled with rapture and happiness, born of concentration. (DN 2.79; emphasis mine)

This does not mean that initial application to the meditation object and sustained application to the meditation object are not a part of the first jhāna. Not only are they an important part of the first jhāna, they are equally important when beginning to meditate in order to generate access concentration. You must initially apply your attention to the meditation object, and in order to generate access concentration, you must sustain your attention on the meditation object. Then to move toward the first jhāna, you must initially find a pleasant sensation and apply your attention to it, and then you sustain your attention on that pleasant sensation until the pīti and sukha arise. Once the pīti and sukha arise, you once again apply and sustain your attention, this time on the pīti-sukha experience.

For the second and higher jhānas, the usual argument from those who understand *vitakka and vicāra* as "initial and sustained application" is that the "unification of mind" that arises in the second jhāna takes over from having to "apply" your attention—your focus becomes automatic, and thus there is no more vitakka and vicāra in the second and higher jhānas. All this is true—but it misses the important point that there is still thinking in the first jhāna, and the subsiding of that thinking is what generates the second jhāna.

If we want to understand what the suttas are saying about the jhānas, it is indeed necessary to understand what the words used actually meant at the time the suttas were composed. *Vitakka* and *vicāra* just mean "thinking," both in the context of the jhānas and throughout the suttas.[4] Understanding this provides a much clearer picture of what the suttas are describing for the first jhāna, as we will see in the next chapter.

12 First Jhāna

Quite secluded from sense pleasures, secluded from unwholesome states, one enters and dwells in the first jhāna, which is accompanied by vitakka and vicāra and filled with pīti and sukha born of seclusion. One drenches, steeps, saturates, and suffuses one's body with this pīti and sukha born of seclusion, so that there is no part of one's entire body which is not suffused by this pīti and sukha. (DN 2.77)

KEY PALI WORDS:

samādhi	indistractability, concentration
vitakka	thinking
vicāra	examining
pīti	glee, rapture
sukha	happiness/joy

"The first jhāna has five factors." The amount of misinformation in that statement is appalling. Those who make such a statement list the following as the five factors:

- vitakka,
- vicāra,
- pīti,

- sukha,
- ekaggata.

A cursory examination of the sutta description of the first jhāna uncovers nothing that could correspond to ekaggata—which means "one-pointedness." When this is pointed out, the usual reply is something like, "It's assumed." Why would it be assumed? An in-depth examination of the sutta description of the first jhāna precludes any possibility of ekaggata being part of the first jhāna—it is simply impossible to have one-pointedness while thinking! The sutta understanding of vitakka and vicāra, explained in the previous chapter, clearly indicates that the first jhāna was not understood as a state of one-pointed absorption.

So how did ekaggata come to be associated with the first jhāna when the description of the first jhāna undeniably precludes such a thing? It appears that, over time, the understanding of what the experience of the first jhāna was changed. Apparently during succeeding generations after the death of the Buddha, the monks* found ways to enter into deeper and deeper meditative states until they reached full absorption, probably long before the *Visuddhimagga* and other commentaries were written, which explicitly describe the first jhāna as an absorption state.

The descriptions of the jhānas found in the Abhidhamma (composed approximately a couple of centuries after the Buddha's death) are different from what is found in the suttas, and that change is consistent with an understanding of the jhānas as more deeply concentrated states.†

* Most likely the nuns were deepening their concentration in the jhānas as well, but since it was monks who wound up composing the later Buddhist literature, I say *monks* rather than *monastics.*

† The Abhidhamma does state that ekaggata is part of *every* mind state—one of the universal cetasikas. This could be the source of this misunderstanding of the sutta description of the first jhāna, but that would be very hard, probably impossible, to determine.

By the time of the *Visuddhimagga* (composed more than eight centuries after the Buddha's death), the first jhāna had come to be understood as a state of full absorption, where not only is thinking not possible, but even hearing and noticing one's body are precluded.[1]

This move toward understanding the first jhāna as a deeper state of concentration is actually hinted at in two passages in a pair of very late suttas. In the Mahāvedalla Sutta (MN 43), we find:

> 18. "Friend, what is the first jhāna?"
>
> "Here, friend, quite secluded from sensual pleasures, secluded from unwholesome states, a bhikkhu enters upon and abides in the first jhāna, which is accompanied by vitakka and vicarā, with pīti and sukha born of seclusion. This is called the first jhāna."

Notice that there are only the usual four "factors" given; there is no mention of *ekaggata* (or *citt'ekaggata*). However, MN 43 is inconsistent—in the next verse, we find:

> 19. "Friend, how many factors does the first jhāna have?"
>
> "Friend, the first jhāna has five factors. Here, when a bhikkhu has entered upon the first jhāna, there occur vitakka, vicarā, pīti, sukha, and citt'ekaggata [one-pointedness of mind]. That is how the first jhāna has five factors."

MN 43 is a "catechism" sutta composed almost entirely of questions and answers. Suttas of this type seem to have been composed long after the Buddha's death when such rote learning was deemed useful for teaching newly ordained monks. This sutta seems to have been composed around the time of the transition from composing suttas to composing the Abhidhamma—it is full of categories and lists. It's not so "late" that there is not a corresponding Chinese āgama;[2] however, in that corresponding āgama, verse 19 is missing. This would imply that verse 19 is a later addition to a late sutta, and the insertion was made without dealing with the inconsistency between verses 18 and 19.[3] This sutta is certainly not a reliable source of information for understanding the jhānas in the bulk of the suttas.

The other place where *ekaggata* is mentioned as a jhāna "factor" comes from the Anupada Sutta (MN 111). Once again we are dealing with a late sutta* that also includes a contradiction:

> 3. "Here, bhikkhus, quite secluded from sensual pleasures, secluded from unwholesome states, Sāriputta entered upon and abided in the first jhāna, which is accompanied by vitakka and vicarā, with pīti and sukha born of seclusion.
>
> 4. "And the states in the first jhāna—the vitakka, vicāra, with pīti, sukha, and citt'ekaggata [one-pointedness of mind]; the contact, feeling, perception, volition, and mind; the zeal, decision, energy, mindfulness, equanimity, and attention—these states were defined by him one by one as they occurred; known to him those states arose, known they were present, known they disappeared.

In verse 3, the standard sutta description of the first jhāna is given—which has no mention of *citt'ekaggata*. Then in verse 4, the sutta says that citt'ekaggata is defined and known along with a host of additional

* See the web page "MN 111" at http://rc.leighb.com/more/MN_111.htm for a detailed discussion of the Anupada Sutta and why it is considered late and unreliable.

factors. These additional factors come to prominence in the Abhidhamma. Caroline Rhys Davids points out that this sutta's style is similar to that of the *Dhammasaṅgaṇī,* regarded as one of the earliest books of the Abhidhamma.[4]* Once again we have a sutta that is certainly not a reliable source of information for understanding the jhānas found in the bulk of the suttas.

So does this mean that the first jhāna as described in the suttas has four factors:

- vitakka,
- vicāra,
- pīti,
- sukha?

What about the mention in the description of the first jhāna of being "secluded from sense pleasures" and "secluded from unwholesome states"? Aren't these actually an important part of generating the first jhāna, especially since pīti and sukha are said to be born of seclusion? Should the first jhāna actually have six factors:

- seclusion from sense pleasures,
- seclusion from unwholesome states,
- vitakka,
- vicāra,
- pīti,
- sukha?

---

* See the web page "Abhidhamma Jhānas" at http://rc.leighb.com/more/Abhidhamma_Jhanas.htm for more information on the view of the jhānas found in the *Dhammasaṅgaṇī.*

But in the chapter "Vitakka and Vicāra," we saw that really vitakka and vicāra are not two distinct things in the sutta description of the first jhāna; they are mentioned as a way of emphasizing that thinking is present. So maybe we are back to five factors:

- seclusion from sense pleasures,
- seclusion from unwholesome states,
- vitakka and vicāra,
- pīti,
- sukha?

But really it's the seclusion itself that is important, not the two things mentioned to be secluded from.* So maybe we are back again to four factors:

- seclusion,
- vitakka and vicāra,
- pīti,
- sukha?

But what does it really mean to be a factor of something? The dictionary definition of *factor* is "something that actively contributes to an accomplishment, result, or process."† Does thinking actually contribute to the experiencing of the first jhāna—or isn't the thinking really just a defect in concentration that doesn't detract from the first jhāna? It

---

* As mentioned in the chapters "Access Concentration" and "First Jhāna," this "seclusion" refers to being secluded from the hindrances.

† The Pali word being translated as "factor" is *aṅga* meaning "a constituent part of a whole or system or collection" or "a constituent part as characteristic, prominent or distinguishing, a mark, attribute, sign, quality" according to the Pali Text Society's dictionary. "Factor" indeed has the same meaning.

seems weird to include a noncontributing defect as a factor! So does this mean the first jhāna only has three factors:

- seclusion,
- pīti,
- sukha?

And what about initial and sustained application/attention to the pīti and sukha? Now we know that *vitakka* and *vicāra* refer to thinking—so how do we factor in the initial and sustained application/attention that are required to enter and remain in the jhāna?

It seems that the whole idea of "factors of the first jhāna" is simply not a useful concept. In fact "jhāna factors" in general is not a concept found in the suttas except in the two above-mentioned late and internally contradictory suttas. And the Pali word *aṅga,* which is translated as "factor" and is used in many places in the suttas, only appears in relation to the jhānas in one place—MN 43.19 (mentioned above).

If we really want to understand what the Buddha was experiencing and teaching for the first jhāna, it's probably better to ignore the word "factor" completely and simply talk about the *qualities mentioned* for the first jhāna, which are four:

- seclusion,
- vitakka and vicāra,
- pīti,
- sukha.

And it is important to remember that this is not a complete list—initial and sustained application/attention to the pīti and sukha are not mentioned in the standard sutta description. However, in the Poṭṭhapāda

Sutta (DN 9.10), we do find the following after the standard first jhāna description: "Having reached the first jhāna, one remains in it. . . . At that time there is present a true but subtle perception of pīti and sukha born of seclusion, and one becomes one who is conscious of this pīti and sukha." (DN 9.10)

If we really want to list the qualities of the first jhāna we could have

- seclusion,
- vitakka and vicāra,
- pīti,
- sukha,
- consciousness of pīti and sukha.

The standard description of the first jhāna goes on to say that once the pīti and sukha are established, they should be spread throughout your body. Again we have textual evidence that the later understanding expressed in the commentaries is simply wrong. As mentioned above, the commentaries describe the first jhāna as having concentration so deep as to generate a state of complete absorption[5]—one where you don't hear sounds or experience any tactile sensations or even are aware of the passage of time. But if there is no body awareness at all, how on earth could you "drench, steep, saturate, and suffuse your body with this pīti and sukha born of seclusion, so that there is no part of your entire body which is not suffused by this pīti and sukha"?

Now, the usual retort from those who understand jhānas based on the commentaries is to point out that the word translated as "body" is *kāya,* which means "group, heap, collection," rather than *rūpa,* which means "materiality." Hence, they say, in English we should read something like "being," and it refers to one's mental being. There is some truth to this in that *kāya* could include one's mental being. But the passage on insight knowledge, which often follows the description of the fourth jhāna, makes it very clear from the context there that *kāya* is being used to refer to the physical body.* The heart of the matter is that the all-pervasive pīti and sukha should be completely encompassing, both mentally and physically. It's quite clear from the sutta description of the first jhāna that not only is its concentration level not deep enough to shut off all thinking, but it also is not deep enough to block tactile awareness.

A final defense of the first jhāna being a state of complete absorption is made by those who favor the interpretation of the jhānas found in the commentaries by quoting from Anguttara-Nikāya 10.72 (Kaṇṭaka Sutta): "Noise is a thorn to the first jhāna." This is interpreted to mean that you can't hear anything when properly in the first jhāna. But take a look at the complete list of ten thorns:

> (1) Delight in company is a thorn to one who delights in solitude. (2) Pursuit of an attractive object is a thorn to one intent on meditation on the mark of the unattractive. (3) An unsuitable show is a thorn to one guarding the doors of the sense faculties. (4) Keeping company with women is a thorn to the celibate life. (5) Noise is a thorn to the first jhāna. (6) Thinking and examining are a thorn to the second jhāna. (7) Rapture is a thorn to the third jhāna. (8) In-and-out breathing is a thorn to the fourth jhāna. (9) Perception and feeling are a thorn to the attainment of the cessation of perception and feeling. (10) Lust is a thorn, hatred is a thorn, and delusion is a thorn.

Each thorn is something that, if attention is given to it, makes it difficult—even impossible—to do something you intend to do. Far from

* See chapter 17, "Insight Knowledge," for a more detailed discussion of *kāya* as "body."

confirming that you don't hear in the first jhāna, it simply confirms the obvious that trying to meditate in a noisy environment is unlikely to lead to concentration deep enough to enter or to sustain the first jhāna.

In summary, what the sutta description of the first jhāna is saying is the following: Become secluded from the hindrances. Don't worry if there is still some background thinking. Pīti and sukha will be generated via the pāmojja (worldly joy) that arises from being secluded from the hindrances. Focus on the pīti and sukha; sustaining them enables you to remain in the first jhāna. Spread the pīti and sukha throughout your body.

13 Second Jhāna

Further, with the subsiding of vitakka and vicāra, one enters and dwells in the second jhāna, which is accompanied by inner tranquility and unification of mind and is without vitakka and vicāra and is filled with pīti and sukha born of concentration. One drenches, steeps, saturates and suffuses one's body with the pīti and sukha born of concentration, so that there is no part of one's entire body not suffused by this pīti and sukha. (DN 2.79)

KEY PALI WORDS:

samādhi indistractability, concentration
vitakka thinking
vicāra examining
pīti glee, rapture
sukha happiness/joy

IN THE SUTTA DESCRIPTION of the jhānas, the point of demarcation between the first and second jhānas occurs when the vitakka and vicāra—the thinking—fully subsides. If you've been paying attention, you might feel this contradicts what I wrote earlier in the chapter on the second jhāna, where I seemed to indicate that the point of demarcation between the first and second jhānas occurs with the foreground-background shift between pīti and sukha. What's going on here? The answer is that what I wrote in the chapter on the second jhāna is for pedagogical purposes.

If we carefully read the suttas' description of the second jhāna, it indicates that three things need to happen:

- the subsiding of vitakka and vicāra,
- [gaining] inner tranquility,
- [gaining] unification of mind.

Now, indeed it is possible to have all three of these occur simultaneously, but if you are trying to learn to move intentionally between the first and second jhāna, this is quite a challenge. So with the instruction to make the foreground-background shift between pīti and sukha by taking a deep breath, you initially work on generating some degree of inner tranquility. Obviously, once the vitakka and vicāra subside completely, the inner tranquility is much more pronounced. But doing the foreground-background shift between pīti and sukha serves two purposes: (1) the pīti, which is sometimes uncomfortably strong, is now brought down to an intensity level that is far more bearable, and (2) the generating of inner tranquility has begun.

Then all that is necessary to complete the process of entering the second jhāna is to stay strongly focused on the (now foreground) sukha until the vitakka and vicāra subside and the mind becomes unified around the sukha-pīti experience. There is nothing really to "do." There is only the patient focusing on the happiness/joy. If the concentration generated while you were in access concentration was strong enough, once the foreground-background shift has been made, the vitakka and vicāra do subside on their own, and the unification of mind arises automatically. The second jhāna has arrived.

So why don't I teach like I described above? Well, from a historical perspective, it's because when I learned the jhānas, to move from the first jhāna to the second was to make the foreground-background shift. It was only much later that I realized exactly what the suttas were saying. Then I understood also that I was indeed actually experiencing the second jhāna as described in the suttas, but it was really only occurring some time after I made the foreground-background shift—it was only when I felt I was getting more strongly into the second jhāna that I was actually just arriving there. This realization dawned on me while I was on a long retreat, so I had lots of occasions to carefully observe what was happening and was able to identify exactly what was going on. But I found there really wasn't a distinct "landmark" that marked the shift from the first to the second jhāna. The post-foreground-background shift part of the first jhāna gave way slowly to a more concentrated state, with the thinking slowly subsiding during that time. When my concentration was really strong, the thinking would completely subside; when my concentration was not as strong, the thinking wouldn't completely go away but would be so intermittent and so far in the background that there was no chance it was going to turn into a distraction.

I definitely considered changing the way I taught the second jhāna but realized that without a good landmark to delineate the end of the first jhāna and the beginning of the second, I was more likely to cause confusion, rather than provide instructions that were more helpful than what I had been teaching previously. Given that the foreground-background shift is helpful in all cases, a student would do well to take to heart the instructions given in the chapter above on the second jhāna:

> If you can remain fully focused on the sukha, really giving yourself to this experience of happiness/joy, the thinking will indeed subside and fade more and more the longer you stay there without becoming distracted. . . .
>
> What you want is sukha that is moderately intense and a mind that is strongly unified around this experience of sukha—in other words, moderate happiness/joy, strong one-pointed focus.

Then one will indeed arrive at the second jhāna as described in the suttas.

Students do report that they sometimes are unsure of which jhāna they are in; they know they are really concentrated but are unable to determine clearly the qualities of the mind state. So having easily distinguishable landmarks that mark the transition points seems to be very helpful. By following the instructions given in the chapter on the second jhāna, a student will both have a distinct landmark, and, as they follow the instructions mentioned above, they will indeed progress into the second jhāna as described in the suttas.

So, yes, I am guilty of being more practical than precise. But since the practical instructions enable a student to achieve the precise results, I'm not going to worry about it.

In the suttas it says that vitakka and vicāra are a thorn to the second jhāna.[1] Once the unification of mind has kicked in and the thinking has subsided, there is no guarantee that the thinking won't return. If it does, you are, by definition, back in the first jhāna. Simply redouble your efforts to be undistractedly focused on the sukha; when the thinking subsides again, and that may be quite quickly, you have reentered the second jhāna. The object of the second jhāna—the sukha, with background pīti*—is more subtle than the not-at-all subtle pīti of the first jhāna. So it does take good concentration to remain in the second jhāna.

In the previous chapter, we saw that the whole idea of "factors of the first jhāna" is simply not a useful concept. Again, for the second jhāna, it is much more accurate to talk about the qualities of the second jhāna rather than its factors. But that didn't stop the Abhidhamma and commentaries from listing the factors of the second jhāna as

---

* In DN 9 (Poṭṭhapāda Sutta), we find that after one makes the transition from the first jhāna to the second, "one's former true but subtle perception of pīti and sukha born of seclusion vanishes. At that time there arises a true but subtle perception of pīti and sukha born of concentration, and one becomes one who is conscious of this pīti and sukha."

- pīti,
- sukha,
- ekaggata.

This of course leaves out the two very important qualities of inner tranquility (ajjhattaṃ sampasādana) and unification of mind (ekodi-bhavam). Why weren't they included? Probably the unification of mind is assumed to be the same as the ekaggata even though they are different words in Pali. But what about the inner tranquility? I can only speculate that adding additional factors goes against the thrust of the jhāna instructions found in the Abhidhamma and commentaries, which basically subtract factors until there are only two factors left—the second one always being ekaggata and the first one changing for each jhāna as one progresses from third jhāna to eighth jhāna.

A correct listing of the qualities of the second jhāna would be

- ajjhattaṃ sampasādana,
- ekodi-bhavam,
- pīti,
- sukha.

But remember: these are best thought of as qualities, not as factors.

In summary, what the sutta description of the second jhāna is saying is the following: Hang out in the first jhāna until your mind calms down. Let the thinking subside as your mind becomes unified around the calmer experience of pīti and sukha. At that point you enter and dwell in the second jhāna, with its inner tranquility and unification of mind. There isn't any thinking and your mind is filled with pīti and sukha, now born of concentration.

14 Third Jhāna

Further, with the fading away of pīti, one dwells in equanimity, mindful and clearly comprehending, and experiences happiness with the body. Thus one enters and dwells in the third jhāna, of which the noble ones declare: "One dwells happily with equanimity and mindfulness." One drenches, steeps, saturates, and suffuses one's body with sukha free from pīti, so that there is no part of one's entire body that is not suffused by this sukha. (DN 2.81)

KEY PALI WORDS:

samādhi	indistractability, concentration
pīti	glee, rapture
sukha	happiness/joy
upekkha	equanimity, literally "gaze upon"
sukha kāyena	bodily happiness

THE PĪTI, which was so strong in the first jhāna and remained in the background of the second jhāna, now fades away completely. The disappearance of the pīti leaves you in a much calmer state—a state that is equanimous. The word *upekkhako* literally means "gaze upon"—with the sense of gazing upon your experience, being fully engaged, and not being disturbed either positively or negatively. This, along with the sukha that remains, leaves you in a state where it is easy to be mindful and clearly comprehend what you are experiencing.

The sutta description also says one experiences bodily happiness (sukha kāyena). The word translated as "bodily" is *kāyena,* literally "by means of the body," and the word *body* (*kāya*) is, as we saw in the discussion of the first jhāna, referring to the physical body. This happiness has arisen due to the pīti fading out—somewhat like the experience of a postorgasmic glow. The suttas mention, "On account of the presence of pīti there is mental exhilaration, and that state is considered gross."[1] The word translated as "mental" is *cetaso,* the genitive of *ceto,* which is derived from *citta,* meaning "heart/mind," and would be as close as Pali comes to describing a "seat of emotions." So to get a more accurate sense of what the description is saying, we can rewrite the phrase "with the fading away of pīti, one . . . experiences happiness with the body" as "with the fading away of pīti (which was producing mental/emotional as well as physical exhilaration), one . . . experiences bodily happiness." And the "drenches, steeps, saturates, and suffuses" ensures that the happiness is throughout one's whole being.

It is not obvious why the sutta description of this jhāna includes "third jhāna, of which the noble ones declare: 'One dwells happily with equanimity and mindfulness.'" None of the other jhāna descriptions contain a quote or anything quite like this. Perhaps since a noble one is one who has achieved awakening, it is saying that the state of awakening is a happy state of equanimity and mindfulness, and that the third jhāna provides a hint of what that mind state might be like.

In the suttas it says that pīti is a thorn to the third jhāna.[2] If the pīti fades away on its own and you slide "automatically" to the third jhāna, the pīti is not likely to return. But if you intentionally move to the third jhāna via the method outlined in the earlier chapter on the third jhāna, there is no guarantee that the pīti won't return. If it does, you are, by definition, back in the second jhāna—no matter how contented the sukha feels. If this happens, it is necessary to reestablish your "normal" second jhāna with its foreground sukha and background pīti; then try again to move to the third jhāna. The object of the third jhāna—the sukha* as contentment—is even more subtle than the sukha as happiness/joy (plus pīti) of the second jhāna. So it does take even better concentration to remain in the third jhāna.

In the chapter on the first jhāna, we saw that the whole idea of "factors of the first jhāna" is simply not a useful concept. Again, for the third jhāna, it is much more accurate to talk about the qualities of the third jhāna rather than its factors. But that didn't stop the Abhidhamma and commentaries from listing the factors of the third jhāna as

- sukha,
- ekaggata.

They completely ignored the equanimity, mindfulness, clear comprehension, and bodily happiness that are so obviously mentioned in the sutta description of the third jhāna. A correct listing of the qualities mentioned for the third jhāna would be

- upekkha,
- sati,
- sampajañña,

* In DN 9 (Poṭṭhapāda Sutta), we find that after one makes the transition from the second jhāna to the third, "one's former true but subtle sense of pīti and sukha born of concentration vanishes, and there arises at that time a true but subtle sense of equanimity and happiness [i.e., contentment], and one becomes one who is conscious of this true but subtle sense of equanimity and happiness."

- sukha kāyena,
- sukha.

But the inner tranquility and unification of mind that were established in the second jhāna still remain even though they are not mentioned. So a complete listing of the qualities of the third jhāna would be

- (ajjhattaṃ sampasādana),
- (ekodi-bhavam),
- upekkha,
- sati,
- sampajañña,
- sukha kāyena,
- sukha.

Unlike the factors described in the Abhidhamma and commentaries, the sutta description and actual experience of the third jhāna yield more, not fewer, qualities than those of the second jhāna.

In summary, what the sutta description of the third jhāna is saying is the following: With the fading away of the exhilarating pīti, one dwells in equanimity, mindful and clearly comprehending, and experiences bodily happiness. Thus one enters and remains in the third jhāna, of which the awakened ones declare: "One dwells happily with equanimity and mindfulness"; one is fully contented.

15 Fourth Jhāna

Further, with the abandoning of sukha and dukkha, and with the previous passing away of somanassa and domanassa, one enters and dwells in the fourth jhāna, which is adukkha and asukha and contains mindfulness fully purified by equanimity. One sits suffusing one's body with a pure bright mind, so that there is no part of one's entire body not suffused by a pure bright mind. (DN 2.81)

KEY PALI WORDS:

samādhi	indistractability, concentration
sukha and dukkha	pleasure and pain
adukkha and asukha	neither painful nor pleasant
somanassa and domanassa	joy and grief
sati	mindfulness
upekkha	equanimity
pārisuddhi	purity

IN THE LATER Abhidhamma and commentaries, *sukha and dukkha* came to mean physical pleasure and pain while *somanassa and domanassa* came to mean mental joy and sorrow. But in the suttas, the meanings of these words are not so fixed. For example, we find *sukha and dukkha* used in the discussion of *vedanā* (feelings or feeling tone),[1] and vedanā are always mental, even though at times they derive from the five external (physical) senses.

So to determine the exact usage of these words in the context of the fourth jhāna, it is necessary to understand both the qualities of the previous jhānas and the target of the fourth jhāna. The most obvious components of the previous jhānas are the pīti and sukha. The pīti, with its exhilarating glee, is present in the first and second jhānas but has "passed away" by the third jhāna. The sukha, with its pleasant joyfulness, has decreased in intensity by the third jhāna but is still present and pleasant.

The target of the fourth jhāna is to be without pleasure and pain and to be equanimous. This indicates that the mind is to become emotionally neutral in the fourth jhāna. Thus the two rhyming phrases (in Pali) "sukhassa and dukkhassa" and "somanassa and domanassa" are used to point toward the neutral state between the extremes mentioned in those phrases, as does the semantically related phrase "adukkha and asukha."

The word *somanassa* derives from *su* + *mano,* meaning "happy mind," the *su* being the same as in *sukha. Somanassa* is a synonym of *veda* according to the Pali Text Society's dictionary. *Veda,* according to the same dictionary, means "(joyful) feeling, religious feeling, enthusiasm, awe, emotion, excitement." The combination of exhilarating pīti and joyful sukha in the first and second jhānas is being referred to here as *somanassa. Domanassa* is just the rhyming opposite of *somanassa* and is being used in contrast so that the combination points to neutrality. The "equanimity and happiness" of the third jhāna is definitely pleasant and is referred to here as *sukhassa.* Its opposite, *dukkhassa* is used again to point to the neutrality of the fourth jhāna. Notice also the alliteration of *sukhassa* and *somanassa* and of *dukkhassa* and *domanassa* and the rhyming *assa* in all four words, which serve to help memorization.[2]

The phrase translated as "contains mindfulness fully purified by equanimity" is *upekkha-sati-pārisuddhim,* which is a triple compound.

Sometimes you will see it translated as "purified by equanimity and mindfulness" rather than "mindfulness fully purified by equanimity." *Upekkha* of course is "equanimity," and *sati* is "mindfulness." *Pārisuddhi* means "purity," but the triple compound could be interpreted multiple ways and justify either of these translations.

The "drenches, steeps, saturates, and suffuses one's body" is now replaced with "sits suffusing one's body," which makes sense given how much more calm the fourth jhāna is.

Notice also that in the previous jhānas, the body is to be suffused with the object of attention; here the body is to be suffused with a new term not previously mentioned: "the pure bright mind" (parisuddhena cetasā pariyodātena). *Cetasā* is "mind," and both of the other words mean "clean, clear, pure." Sometimes the phrase *parisuddhena cetasā pariyodātena* is translated as "mental purity and clarification." Either way it is certainly pointing to a subtle, unruffled mind state.

In the suttas it says that in-and-out breathing is a thorn to the fourth jhāna.[3] This is misinterpreted by the later literature to mean that one ceases to breath in the fourth jhāna.* This is quite absurd—people who quit breathing soon become dead! What it actually means is that in the fourth jhāna, things are so quiet and still, and the object of your attention is so subtle, that your breathing can become distracting. Of course the later literature could not interpret this thorn that way since the later literature claims that even in the first jhāna, one is so deeply absorbed as to have no bodily awareness.

Again, for the fourth jhāna, it is much more accurate to talk about the qualities of the fourth jhāna rather than its factors. But that didn't

---

*Johannes Bronkhorst (*The Two Traditions of Meditation in Ancient India*, 1993) and Grzegorz Polak (*Reexamining Jhāna: Towards a Critical Reconstruction of Early Buddhist Soteriology*, 2011) feel that this later idea of stopping the in- and out-breaths is due to influence from both Jain and early Hindu meditation techniques.

stop the Abhidhamma and commentaries from listing the factors of the fourth jhāna as

- upekkha,
- ekaggata.

Why isn't sati (mindfulness) one of the factors? Perhaps since they considered mindfulness to be a factor for all wholesome states, they didn't feel a need to mention it. But they also considered ekaggata to be a factor of all mental states, so that conjecture makes no sense since they explicitly list it for each of the jhānas.

The neither pleasant nor painful quality (adukkha and asukha) is the object of attention in the fourth jhāna,* so certainly it is a very important quality of the fourth jhāna. The actual qualities mentioned in the usual sutta description of the fourth jhāna are

- adukkha and asukha,
- upekkha,
- sati.

The more elaborate sutta descriptions of the fourth jhāna also mention "the pure bright mind," so that would give us

- adukkha and asukha,
- upekkha,
- sati,
- parisuddhena cetasā pariyodātena.

* In the Poṭṭhapāda Sutta (DN 9.13), we find that after one makes the transition from the third jhāna to the fourth, "one's former true but subtle sense of equanimity and happiness vanishes, and there arises a true but subtle sense of neither pleasure nor pain, and one becomes one who is conscious of this true but subtle sense of neither pleasure nor pain."

And again, there seem to be important qualities of mind that were developed in the earlier jhānas that would still be qualities of the fourth jhāna: the inner tranquility and unification of mind established in the second jhāna and the clear comprehension established in the third jhāna. So a complete listing of the qualities of the fourth jhāna would be

- (ajjhattaṃ sampasādana),
- (ekodi-bhavam),
- (sampajañña),
- adukkha and asukha,
- upekkha,
- sati,
- parisuddhena cetasā pariyodātena.

The qualities may be numerous, but the actual experience is very simple: undistracted quiet stillness.

In summary, what the sutta description of the fourth jhāna is saying is the following: With the abandoning of the pleasure of the third jhāna, and with the previous passing away of the joyful excitement of the first and second jhānas, one enters and dwells in the fourth jhāna, which is emotionally neutral and contains mindfulness fully purified by equanimity. One sits suffusing one's body with a pure bright mind, so that there is no part of one's entire body not suffused by a pure bright mind.

16 The Jhāna Summary

When one sees that these five hindrances have been abandoned within oneself, gladness arises. From gladness, rapture arises. When one's mind is filled with rapture, one's body becomes tranquil; tranquil in body, one experiences happiness; being happy, one's mind becomes concentrated. (DN 2.76)

KEY PALI WORDS:

pāmojja	gladness
pīti	glee, rapture
passaddhakāya	bodily tranquility
sukha	happiness/joy
samādhi	indistractability, concentration

THE ABOVE PERICOPE,* or something quite similar to it, appears in a number of suttas.[1] In the detailed description of the gradual training, it is found between the abandoning of the hindrances and the description of the first jhāna. Now that we've gained an understanding of exactly what is being referred to in the jhāna description found in the suttas, we can unpack this pericope.

The commentaries go to great length to explain how this pericope is

* A pericope is a "stock passage" of text that forms one coherent unit or thought.

showing what happens between the abandoning of the hindrances and the onset of the first jhāna. They discuss how it shows both access concentration and absorption concentration. They indicate that everything from the abandoning of the hindrances through the happiness is access concentration, and then becoming concentrated is absorption concentration. The gladness is identified with showering pīti and is said to be "tender pīti." Because the word *kāyo* is associated with the tranquility, the tranquility is said to be mental since *kāya* means "group, heap, collection" and thus refers to one's being and hence can be interpreted as mental tranquility.[2]

However, the commentaries have completely missed the mark! The abandoning of the hindrances, the pericope above, and the jhāna descriptions are *not* three things in a linear progression. What actually is there is the abandoning of the hindrances, a summary of the whole arc of jhānic experience, and then a full detailed description of the jhānas. A similar pattern occurs earlier in the gradual training. Right after a householder goes forth, there is a summary of the sīla practices: "Having gone forth, one dwells restrained by the restraint of the rules, ... with the sense-doors guarded, skilled in mindful awareness and content."[3] This is followed by a detailed description of the precepts, guarding the senses, mindful awareness, and contentment. The context there makes it very clear it is just a summary.

Most likely this pericope is a late insertion into the gradual training: it's certainly missing a context that makes it clear that it is a summary, it is redundant, it doesn't occur in all recensions of the gradual training, and it seems to have been lifted from other suttas, particularly from the Saṃyutta Nikāya.

The key words also point to this pericope being a summary:

- gladness (pāmojja),
- rapture (pīti),

- bodily tranquility (passaddhakāya),
- happiness (sukha),
- concentration (samādhi).

The gladness occurs prior to the arising of the first jhāna—it arises due to the abandoning of the hindrances. Or to put it another way, the gladness arises when access concentration has been established.* "From gladness, rapture arises." As mentioned in the chapter "Entering the Jhānas," you generate pīti by focusing on a pleasant sensation without becoming distracted and thereby set up a positive feedback loop of pleasure that eventually erupts in pīti-sukha. The enjoyment of the pleasant sensation I'm instructing you to put your attention on after having firmly established access concentration is precisely what is being referred to by this *gladness*. I have not found anyone else, either ancient or modern, noting this key point for entering the first jhāna.

Pīti is the primary quality of the first jhāna and persists less intensely in the second jhāna, where inner tranquility (ajjhattaṃ sampasādana) arises. This inner tranquility is not mentioned in the jhāna summary; it is not the same words as the bodily tranquility (passaddhakāya) that is mentioned.

With the ceasing of the pīti at the onset of the third jhāna, bodily tranquility (passaddhakāya) is experienced. The commentaries could be right in interpreting *kāyo* as "being," in which case this could very well be referring to the mental "inner tranquility" that arises with the subsiding of vitakka and vicāra (thinking) at the onset of the second jhāna. Almost certainly *kāyo* does refer to the physical body as well, if

---

*Abandoning the hindrances is only one of a number of descriptions mentioned in the suttas of establishing access concentration. See for example the Mahānāma Sutta at AN 11.12 for six recollection practices that establish access concentration and are followed by this jhāna summary.

not exclusively. With the pīti gone, one "experiences happiness with the body," exactly as is mentioned in the description of the third jhāna. And as also mentioned above, this is like the experience of a postorgasmic glow. Anyone who has experienced "all-pervasive" pīti immediately realizes that the experience of such intense pīti has nothing in common with bodily tranquility. The only way bodily tranquility can arise is if the pīti ceases—and that is exactly what happens. And not just as the pīti ceases: the bodily tranquility is actually generated by the deflating of the excited pīti energy.

Now with things calmed down, you can rest in the primary experience of the third jhāna, which is contentment—sukha infused with equanimity and mindfulness. After letting your mind grow even more settled, you abandon the pleasure of the third jhāna and sink down into the deep concentration of the fourth jhāna.

We can now construct the following table:

- abandoning the hindrances—access concentration
- gladness (pāmojja)—focusing on the pleasant sensation
- rapture (pīti)—first and second jhānas
- bodily tranquility (passaddhakāya)—second and third jhānas
- happiness (sukha)—third jhāna (the pīti is gone since passaddhakāya precedes this; therefore, third jhāna only)
- concentration (samādhi)—fourth jhāna

A very similar progression of "gladness, rapture, tranquility, happiness, concentration, knowing & seeing things as they are" occurs in the Upanisā Sutta (SN 12.23) with each item being dependent upon the previous. However, there tranquility is *passaddhi,* with no reference to any *kāya.* This sequence could very well be interpreted as "gladness, first jhāna, second jhāna, third jhāna, fourth jhāna, and knowing and seeing things as they are," the latter being insight/wisdom. This again points to our pericope being a jhāna summary.

Now, I have to admit, I figured out that I was entering the first jhāna by establishing access concentration and then focusing on a pleasant sensation more than a decade before I realized the paragraph here is a jhāna summary that contains valuable information about entering and moving between the jhānas. The information given in the suttas is so terse that you pretty much have to be skilled in the jhānas before you can puzzle out what the suttas are actually describing. But once you do understand what they are describing, you find the jhānas described in the suttas to be concentration states that are accessible by many people and can furthermore turbocharge their insight practice.

17 Insight Knowledge

When one's mind is thus concentrated, pure and bright, unblemished, free from defects, malleable, wieldy, steady and attained to imperturbability, one directs and inclines it to knowing and seeing. One understands thus, this is my body, having material form, composed of the four primary elements, originating from mother and father, built up out of rice and gruel, impermanent, subject to rubbing and pressing, to dissolution and dispersion, and this is my consciousness, supported by it and bound up with it. (DN 2.83)

THE PALI WORD translated as "body" in the above description of insight practice is *kāya* and is clearly referring to the physical body since it is said to be *rūpī* and *cātummahābhūtiko,* meaning "having material form and composed of the four primary elements." This is the same as the body (kāya) that one is to drench, steep, saturate, and suffuse.

This body is to be investigated from several angles. It is to be seen as material and constructed from the elements via nutriment. This body had a beginning, and because it is impermanent, it will come to an end—and along the way it will be subject to dukkha. These investigations are helpful to see the body's impermanent nature and help bring about disidentification with it. In a number of suttas,[1] the Buddha points out that something that is impermanent and dukkha is not worthy of being thought of as "my self." This leads to disenchantment (i.e., dispels the enchantment) with the body, which is one of the steps necessary for being able to let go sufficiently to achieve awakening.

The word translated as "consciousness" is *viññāna*. *Viññāna* is used in many different ways in the suttas—as a synonym for "mind," as "sense consciousness," as one of the five aggregates, as the sixth element.[2] Here, *viññāna* is being used synonymously for "mind" as a counterpart to *kāya* for "body." This usage is fairly rare in the suttas—the most common way of referring to "mind and body" is *nāma-rūpa*.* The rarity of this usage and the pervasive usage of *nāma-rūpa* would tend to indicate that this particular paragraph (pericope, actually) is an early composition.

What you are to notice about your mind is that it is supported by and bound up with your body. This phrase and the Buddha's rebuke of Sati (who believed his consciousness transmigrated at death) in the Mahātaṇhāsaṅkhaya Sutta (MN 38) are two of the clearest indications that the Buddha did not teach reincarnation. Your consciousness/mind is a dependent phenomenon, dependent on your impermanent body. This impermanent consciousness is not worthy of being thought of as "my self," and again this leads to disenchantment.

In the suttas, there is a simile given for insight knowledge: "It is just as if there were a gem, a beryl, pure, excellent, well cut into eight facets, clear, bright, unflawed, perfect in every respect, strung on a blue, yellow, red, white or orange cord. A man with good eyesight, taking it in his hand and inspecting it, would describe it as such" (DN 2.86).

Clear beryl is very transparent, and it would be very easy to see the thread inside the gem. This seeing into is of course what we mean by *insight*. The concentrated, post-jhānic mind is well suited to examine the reality of body and mind and see into the deeper truths available when looking from a less egocentric perspective.

* *Nāma-rūpa* would more accurately be translated as "mentality and materiality."

18 The Immaterial States

Four things which were perfectly proclaimed by the Lord . . . [include] . . . four āruppa. (DN 33 1.11.7)

THE WORD *āruppa* would be best translated as "immaterial states." These "higher attainments" are never referred to in the suttas as *jhānas,* although they are mentioned in a large number of suttas. Sometimes they are discussed by themselves; sometimes they are combined with the four jhānas to make a sequence of eight states of concentration. In later literature they came to be known as the "four immaterial jhānas"—the *arūpa jhānas.* The four jhānas of the suttas were then referred to as *rūpa jhānas.* This was a quite handy innovation because now the word *jhāna* could be used to refer to all eight states. *Rūpa* or *arūpa* could then be prefixed to designate the four jhānas or the four immaterial states when such a distinction needed to be made.

The Pali word *rūpa* means "materiality." The choice of *rūpa* probably was made based on it being the semantic opposite of *arūpa,* which was already being used to refer to the immaterial states. These four rūpa jhānas are obviously not material; they are mental states. But there are valid reasons to refer to the four jhānas of the suttas as *rūpa jhānas.* Certainly in the first jhāna, there is a material component, since the pīti is strongly felt in the body. Also for each of these four jhānas, the suttas say something like, "One drenches, steeps, saturates, and suffuses one's body." Clearly in the rūpa jhānas, you are still aware of your material body: you can feel the rapture in your body; you can spread the qualities throughout your body; you experience the happiness with your body in the third jhāna.

Another quality of the rūpa jhānas is that these are experiences that we have had in the material world. We've all experienced rapture, happiness, contentment, and equanimity. But in the rūpa jhānas, these are more refined states, so they are sometimes called "fine (or refined) material jhānas." In contrast, the experiences of the four arūpa states are unlike anything we have experienced in the material world.

Sometimes people want to make the immaterial states into an experience of tapping into an ontologically existent infinite space, infinite consciousness, realm of nothingness, and/or realm of neither perception nor nonperception. It's true that in later Buddhism, there came to be the understanding that these states were a "visit" to 4 of the 31 realms of existence. And in pre-Buddhist Brahmanism, this seems to be the assumption, given the Buddha-to-be's comments in the Ariyapariyesanā Sutta (MN 26.15–16) that the last two of these states led only to reappearance in the corresponding realm. But the early sutta understanding is not that these states corresponded to any ontologically existent realms—the Buddha of the early suttas is portrayed as a phenomenologist, not a metaphysicist.

The Buddha was often asked a ten-point "questionnaire" about his teachings. This included "Is the cosmos infinite or not?" He refused to give an answer to any of these questions, saying that they were "not conducive to the purpose, not conducive to Dhamma, not the way to embark on the holy life."[1] In other words, trying to obtain answers to these questions was a waste of time and energy. But had the Buddha felt that the experience of the realm of infinite space (ākāsānañcāyatana) was an experience of something that is ontologically existent, there would be no effort needed to confirm that the cosmos was infinite, and he could have immediately answered that the cosmos is indeed infinite.* His refusal to answer the question one way or the other would imply that he did not think he was experiencing an ontologically existent infinite space in the first of the immaterial states.

In the Mahātaṇhāsaṅkhaya Sutta (MN 38), when speaking to Sati (who held a wrong view of consciousness), several monks insist, "In many ways the Blessed One has stated consciousness to be dependently arisen, since without a condition there is no origination of consciousness." Sati's wrong view was not that there is an ontologically existent infinite consciousness, but the Buddha's reasons for categorically rejecting Sati's view also apply here. In the teachings of dependent origination, consciousness is said to be dependently arisen. In some suttas it is said to originate dependent on mind and body (nāma-rūpa);[2] in others it arises dependent on fabrications (sankhara).[3] This is not a contradiction; it's simply that consciousness arises dependent on more than one thing—just like many things in the world. What is important is to realize that no consciousness is independently, ontologically existent. Consciousness only arises dependent on a mind and a sense organ plus an object of that consciousness. The realm of infinite consciousness (viññāṇañcāyatana) of the second immaterial state, for all its infiniteness, is still a consciousness and cannot have independent existence. Postulating a dependent ontologically existent external infinite consciousness that can be tapped into doesn't help either. It would require some mind to be always hanging around generating this infinite consciousness—and that's beginning to sound a lot like postulating the existence of an eternal God, which the Buddha clearly rejected.

Both of these experiences are just mental experiences that are per-

* The Pali word *ananta* (infinite) is used in reference to both "infinite space" and "infinite cosmos."

ceived* as an experience of something external and infinite. Misperceptions abound, and on the spiritual path, it is very important not to be fooled by them.

Given that the first two immaterial states are only mental experiences that are perceived in a way that makes them seem external, it is also quite likely that the third of these states, the realm of nothingness (ākiñcaññāyatana), is also just an experience and not a tapping into some ontologically existent nothingness. However, unlike the previous two states, there is nothing in the Buddha's teachings that can easily be used to point to the existence or nonexistence of some ontologically existent nothingness. Given this lack of sutta material, attempting to prove there is or is not some external ontologically existent realm of nothingness would "not [be] conducive to the purpose, not conducive to Dhamma, not the way to embark on the holy life."

If on the other hand, as some scholars propose, these immaterial states were inserted into the suttas at a later time,[4] the question of whether or not they correspond to ontologically existent realms becomes moot. The questions now become who did these insertions, what was their agenda, and what was their belief system? A detailed discussion of this proposition is beyond the scope of the present work.

The phrase translated as "the realm of neither perception nor non-perception" is the Pali phrase *nevasaññānāsaññāyatana.* The word *sañña* is usually translated as "perception," meaning the ability to name or identify the object of sensory input. But *sañña* can also mean "consciousness"—it certainly appears to have that meaning in the Poṭṭhapāda Sutta (DN 9) and perhaps also in the Kalahavivāda Sutta (Snp 4.11). The *Pali-English Dictionary* gives both "consciousness" and "perception" as meanings, and, under meaning number 3, indicates that

* The Pali word *sañña* applies here—"naming," "identifying," "conceptualizing."

nevasaññānāsaññāyatana should be translated as "neither consciousness nor unconsciousness." In "The Origin of Buddhist Meditation," Alexander Wynne provides a long discussion of *nevasaññānāsaññāyatana* as a pre-Buddhist meditative state.[5] From that discussion, it seems quite possible that the correct translation of *nevasaññānāsaññāyatana* should be "the realm of neither consciousness nor unconsciousness."

Unfortunately, getting the name of this state correct still does not provide any more possible way to describe it. The mind is energized (this is not "sinking mind"!) and very clear, but it is not possible to describe the object of concentration other than to say "the mind is in a state that you can't describe." And again, there is no early sutta material that would indicate that the Buddha taught that this was an ontologically existent realm.

19 The Cessation of Perception and Feeling

"Mental activity is worse for me, lack of mental activity is better. If I were to think and imagine, these perceptions [that I have attained] would cease, and coarser perceptions would arise in me. Suppose I were not to think or imagine?" So one neither thinks nor imagines. And then, for one, just these perceptions arise, but other, coarser perceptions do not arise. One attains cessation. (DN 9.17)

THERE IS ANOTHER STATE of very deep concentration called "the cessation of perception and feeling (saññāvedayitanirodha)." In the Poṭṭhapāda Sutta (DN 9), Poṭṭhapāda, who is an ascetic from another sect, wants to know about abhisaññānirodha—literally "higher perception cessation"—which is just another name for saññāvedayitanirodha. This state of cessation is sometimes referred to in later literature as the *ninth jhāna,* but this term seems to produce more confusion than clarity. It is true that in the suttas, attaining the jhānas and immaterial states in sequence from one to either seven or eight is used to generate the concentration necessary to enter this state. But it is a state of suspended animation and quite unlike any of the four jhānas or four immaterial states.

Sometimes this state is referred to with just the word *nirodha.* The Pali word *nirodha* means "cessation" and occurs in several contexts, so it is important to identify exactly what is being referred to when it is used without any qualifiers. Among the contexts are the following:

- a deep concentration state—saññāvedayitanirodha
- the cessation of the fires of greed, hatred, and delusion—synonymous with full awakening, *nibbāna*
- the truth of cessation—the third noble truth of the cessation of dukkha
- cessation in dependent origination—the ceasing of each "link" generating the ceasing of the next link
- cessation as the fifteenth step of the sixteen steps of mindfulness of breathing
- cessation in the phrase "disenchantment, dispassion, cessation, calm, higher knowledge, enlightenment, Nibbāna" (e.g., DN 9.30)
- cessation as the "experience without an experiencer" of a path moment—described in the sixteen insight knowledges of the progress of insight found in the *Visuddhimagga*[1]

It is definitely recommended that the word *nirodha* not be used without qualifiers until it is clear that all parties understand just what context is being referred to.

The state of saññāvedayitanirodha is mentioned in a number of suttas,[2] perhaps most famously in the Mahāparinibbāna Sutta (DN 16) where the Buddha indicates at verse 2.25 that "it is only when the Tathāgata withdraws his attention from outward signs, and by the cessation of certain feelings, enters into the signless concentration of mind, that his body knows comfort" and again in verse 6.8 where the Buddha enters the cessation of perception and feeling as he is dying.

In the Cūḷasuññata Sutta (MN 121), at verse 11 the Buddha describes attaining full awakening based on "attending to the singleness dependent on the signless concentration of mind." The commentaries do not recognize "the signless concentration of mind" as being the same as the cessation of perception and feeling, but possibly they are mistaken. It seems that one emerging from the cessation of perception and feeling has the ability to watch the world and one's self reassemble and from that gains the realization necessary for full awakening.

But entering the cessation of perception and feeling requires extremely deep concentration. It is said that nonreturners and arahats* can enter this state for up to a week. This is usually misinterpreted that only nonreturners and arahats can enter this state,[3] but that does not seem to be the case. However, it may be that only someone who is that spiritually advanced can enter this state for as long as a week.

The award-winning documentary *Short Cut to Nirvana*—a documentary about the Indian Kumbh Mela spiritual festival[4]—contains a scene where a Japanese woman climbs down a ladder into a deep pit. The ladder is withdrawn, and the pit is covered in roofing tin and then dirt. Three days later there is another scene where the dirt and roofing tin are removed, and she climbs out all smiles. She seemingly had to have been in the state of cessation of perception and feeling—suspended animation.

On a trip to Thailand in 1988, I was there for the Thai New Year's festival, which takes place in the spring at the end of the hot season and the beginning of the rainy season. This is "spring cleaning" time. Originally water was captured after it had been poured over the Buddha statues to clean them, and then this "blessed" water was used to give good fortune to one's elders by gently pouring it on their shoulders. Among young people the holiday evolved to include dousing strangers with water (supposedly to relieve the heat). This has further evolved into water fights and splashing water over people riding in vehicles. It's quite a participatory festival to say the least!

I walked down to the main square in Chiang Mai on the first day of

---

* Those at the third stage of awakening or fully awakened.

the festival. It was quite a chaotic scene with people throwing water at each other, onto passing motorcycles, and into the windows of passing cars and buses. But off to one side, out of the way of the water throwing, a small pavilion had been set up. There was a monk seated in full lotus posture in the pavilion, obviously in deep meditation. His eyes were open and downcast, and he had the most serene look on his face I'd ever seen. He was clearly not disturbed by all the chaos happening around him. He was there that afternoon when the big parade came by. He was there that night when they held the first round of the beauty pageant on a stage 30 yards away. He was there the second day, all day and into the evening. He was still there on the third morning. He looked a little tired—serenely tired. He was there that afternoon when the biggest parade of all came by. He was still there that night during the final round of the beauty pageant. He was gone the next morning. He had to have been in saññāvedayitanirodha. There is no way someone could serenely sit without moving in the midst of all that chaos unless they had entered into such a deep state of concentration. It was quite inspiring.

It has been mentioned earlier that there seems to be quite a difference in the understanding of exactly what constitutes the jhānic states between what is described in the suttas and what is described in the later Abhidhamma and commentaries. The *Visuddhimagga* describes the first jhāna in such a way that it is a state of nonperception. There are no body sensations; no sounds are heard; there is not even the sense of time passing.[5] Now this is very different from the description of the suttas where one not only has body awareness but even "drenches, steeps, saturates and suffuses one's body with the pīti and sukha." In fact, the description of the first jhāna in the *Visuddhimagga* sounds quite a bit like a state of no feeling and no perception: saññāvedayitanirodha. This correspondence has been pointed out by Roderick Bucknell in his very interesting article "Reinterpreting the Jhānas."[6]

I personally don't have much experience with the *Visuddhimagga* jhānas. But I do have a bit. I have attended two long retreats with the Venerable Pa Auk, who teaches exactly what is described in the *Visuddhimagga*. During the second one, after being on retreat for almost five months, I did enter a state where there was no feeling, no perception, no body sensations, no sounds, and no passage of time. My approach to this state corresponded step by step exactly to what is found in the *Visuddhimagga,* and it was later confirmed to be the first jhāna. But my experience also exactly matches what is described in the suttas for the cessation of perception and feeling. This state is attainable—with lots of deep practice. But since I was only able to get there once, I have no real experience of its usefulness for gaining insight into the nature of reality.

20 The Psychic Powers

> *When one's mind is thus concentrated, . . . one directs and inclines it to wielding the various kinds of supernormal powers. (DN 2.87)*

In addition to describing how to use your jhānically concentrated mind to gain insight into body and mind, the gradual training describes, in its more detailed recensions, being able to wield various psychic powers (iddhi). These six powers can be divided into three groups of two each, which we will examine in turn.

The first group consists of the mind-made body and the various kinds of supernormal powers. The mind-made body is described thus:

> When one's mind is thus concentrated, pure and bright, unblemished, free from defects, malleable, wieldy, steady and attained to imperturbability, one directs and inclines it to creating from this body another body having form, mind-made, with all its limbs, lacking no faculty. (DN 2.85)

It's not really clear what is going on here. But there is a simile:

> Just as though a man were to pull out a reed from its sheath and think thus: "This is the sheath, this is the reed; the sheath is one, the reed is another; it is from the sheath that the reed has been

> pulled out"; or just as though a man were to pull out a sword from its scabbard and think thus: "This is the sword, this is the scabbard; the sword is one, the scabbard another; it is from the scabbard that the sword has been pulled out"; or just as though a man were to pull a snake out of its slough and think thus: "This is the snake, this is the slough; the snake is one, the slough another; it is from the slough that the snake has been pulled out." (DN 2.86)

Well, that didn't help much. Let's skip it for the moment and examine wielding the various supernormal powers:

> When one's mind is thus concentrated, . . . one directs and inclines it to wielding the various kinds of supernormal powers: being one, one becomes many; having been many, they become one; one appears and vanishes; one goes unhindered through walls, through enclosures, through mountains, as though through space; one dives in and out of the earth as though it were water; one walks on water without sinking as though it were earth; seated cross-legged, one travels in space like birds; with one's hands one touches and strokes the moon and sun so powerful and mighty; one wields bodily mastery even as far as the Brahma-world. (DN 2.87)

You can take this as literally true—but if you do, you might want to skip to the end of this chapter; I have a background in science, and I'm not buying it.

I had an interesting conversation with a student who is very skilled in lucid dreaming—a dream in which you are aware that you are dreaming. He mentioned that not only can you control what happens in a lucid dream—like being able to fly—but also that it is possible, with training, to go from a waking state directly into a lucid dream. In other words, you don't have to fall asleep, wait until you start dreaming, and then recognize you are dreaming. You can train yourself in what is called the *WILD technique:* wake induced lucid dreaming. Is this what is being talked about in the description of the mind-made body? It certainly makes sense—emerging from the fourth jhāna, you have exactly the type of preliminary mind state that the instructions for WILD recommend: quiet, calm, relaxed, not distractable. This would be a great jumping off point for entering a lucid dream. And when you have manifested that lucid dream, you can walk on water, dive into the earth, pass through walls and ramparts unimpeded, and fly through the air—just like in the description of the various kinds of supernormal powers.

There is even a sutta that strongly hints at the powers being solitary. In Anguttara-Nikāya 3.60, the Buddha is having a conversation with the brahmin Saṅgārava. After some discussion of these various kinds of powers, Saṅgārava says, "Only the one who performs this wonder experiences it and it occurs only to him." This is totally congruent with these supernormal powers being a lucid dream. One can learn to enter such dreams via the mind-made body, which is known today as *WILD.*

Like the investigation of your body and mind in the post-jhānic state, these supernormal powers also provide insight—not so much into the nature of reality, but rather into the dreamlike quality of reality. We have a very strong tendency to ignore many of the subtle qualities of reality and just accept that what we perceive is the way things really are. But having gained mastery of lucid dreaming, you would certainly become more aware that just because you perceive something, it doesn't make it reality. The Buddha clearly is not an idealist,* but he definitely does

* Idealism asserts that reality, or reality as we can know it, is fundamentally mental, mentally constructed, or otherwise immaterial.

not want us blindly trusting our perceptions, especially those of a permanent, ultimately satisfying reality full of separately existing entities.*†

> When one's mind is thus concentrated, . . . one directs and inclines it to the divine ear element, which is purified and surpasses the human, one hears both kinds of sounds, the divine and the human, those that are far as well as near. (DN 2.91)
>
> When one's mind is thus concentrated, . . . one directs and inclines it to understanding the minds of others, having encompassed them with their own minds. (DN 2.93)

The next two psychic powers correspond to what today we call *ESP*—extra sensory perception. There are ongoing arguments between those who believe ESP is real and those who think people are just misunderstanding their experiences. We can assign these two powers as being manifestations of what we call *ESP* without having to decide on the scientific validity of ESP. There is certainly something going on among those who believe in ESP, and whether they are just fooling themselves or are actually tapping into something that science is unable to measure is actually irrelevant for explaining these powers—they are what we today call *ESP*. The first one corresponds to what we call "clairaudience" and the second to "reading someone's mind."

Again, whether or not ESP is scientifically valid, insight can be gained from practicing these two powers—insight into the fact that we are not as separate as it visually appears. Albert Einstein has a wonderful quote about our blindness to this interrelatedness:

---

* See SN 12.15 for more on the Buddha's teaching of the middle way between existence and nonexistence.

† For an interesting article on lucid dreams and virtual reality, see "Lucid Dreams, the Original Virtual Reality" at http://elevr.com/lucid-dreams-the-original-virtual-reality/.

> A human being is part of a whole, called by us the "Universe," a part limited in time and space. He experiences himself, his thoughts and feelings, as something separated from the rest—a kind of optical delusion of his consciousness. The striving to free oneself from this delusion is the one issue of true religion. Not to nourish the delusion but to try to overcome it is the way to reach the attainable measure of peace of mind.[1]

The last pair of psychic powers have to do with the always touchy subject of rebirth:

> When one's mind is thus concentrated, . . . one directs and inclines it to recollecting their manifold past lives, that is, one birth, two births, three births, four births, five births, ten births, twenty births, thirty births, forty births, fifty births, a hundred births, a thousand births, a hundred thousand births, many aeons of world-contraction, many aeons of world-expansion, many aeons of world-contraction and expansion: "There I was so named, of such a clan, with such an appearance, such was my nutriment, such my experience of pleasure and pain, such my life-term; and passing away from there, I reappeared elsewhere; and there too I was so named . . . and passing away from there, I reappeared here." (DN 2.95)
>
> When one's mind is thus concentrated, . . . one directs and inclines it to the divine eye, which is purified and surpasses the human, they see beings passing away and reappearing, inferior and superior, fair and ugly, fortunate and unfortunate. They understand how beings pass on according to their actions. (DN 2.97)

In a number of suttas,[2] it says the Buddha, on the night of his awakening, after moving through the four jhānas, spent the first watch of the night remembering his previous births as described in this power. Because India is near the equator, a night there is about 12 hours long all year round. Since there are three watches of the night, the length of each watch is about four hours. If we "do the math" and compute how long the Buddha-to-be had to remember each of a hundred thousand births, it comes to one-seventh of a second.* He had to remember eight things about each birth in one-seventh of a second and repeat that in the next one-seventh of a second and so on nonstop for four hours. The human mind can only process at most about 40 conscious moments per second.[3] If he had to know eight pieces of information in one-seventh of a second, that's 56 conscious moments per second—and we haven't even addressed the "many aeons," whatever that number might be. And you can't say, "He's the Buddha!" because that won't happen for another four to eight hours. So it seems we cannot take the description of remembering past lives literally, at least for the Buddha on the night of his awakening.

The suttas also describe the Buddha practicing the last of these psychic powers, the divine eye, during the second watch of the night on the night of his awakening. This pair of psychic powers are referred to as *true knowledges.* They, along with the third true knowledge of the ending of the āsavas (discussed in the next chapter), make up the "three true knowledges" of Buddhism, in contrast to the "three knowledges" (Three Vedas: Rig, Yajur, Sama) of Brahmanism.

These two psychic post-jhānic activities actually occur more often in the suttas than directing and inclining the jhānically concentrated mind to knowing and seeing. Presumably both of these psychic powers give you insight into impermanence, not-self, and the workings of karma.

---

*4 hours = 4 × 60 minutes = 4 × 60 × 60 seconds = 14,400 seconds. 14,400 ÷ 100,000 = 0.144 or one-seventh of a second per birth.

It appears that after the parinibbāna of the Buddha, two factions arose in the saṅgha: one was made up of "dhamma specialists" who adopted a predominantly cognitive approach to the dhamma; the others were meditators, who practiced the four jhānas, the four immaterial states, and the psychic powers. The Cunda Sutta at AN 6.46 urges harmony between the factions, and there are other suttas that also seem to hint at this split.[4] It seems the dhamma specialists favored the teaching on the five aggregates and were apparently practicing sīla and paññā while the meditators were practicing sīla, samādhi, and iddhi. Apparently harmony between the factions was restored, because we find both plenty of examples of suttas where people reach awakening via insight into the five aggregates* and plenty of examples where people (most frequently mentioned is the Buddha) reach awakening via practicing these last two psychic powers plus the ending of the āsavas.† This may account for the predominance in the Pali canon of practicing these three true knowledges over directing and inclining the jhānically concentrated mind to knowing and seeing.‡

There is a Tibetan story about a young man who studied for many years with a master. Finally his teacher told him it was time to go off on

---

* In fact we find suttas where the five aggregates seem to have been stuffed into an existing sutta in a way that actually doesn't make a whole lot of sense—see for example DN 14.2.22 and SN 12.23.

† Both Bronkhorst (*Two Traditions,* section 8.4.3, p. 78 and section 9.2.7, p. 93ff) and Polak (*Reexamining Jhāna,* 103) feel that these two psychic powers were inserted during a later period into the original text of the Buddha's awakening.

‡ Bronkhorst (*Two Traditions,* section 9.2.7, p. 93) points to a Sūtra of the Sarvastivadins (MĀc p. 589c14–23) in which the account of the Buddha's liberation is without these two psychic powers. He feels that the account of the Buddha's liberation originally made no mention of his earlier lives and of the knowledge of the births and deaths of beings. On page 94 he writes, "Schmithausen (1981: 221–22, n. 75) comes to the same conclusion, also basing himself on texts which describe the way to salvation for others than the Buddha. The *Madhyama Āgama* (T. 26), Schmithausen observes, seems to have fewer accounts *with* memory of earlier lives and knowledge of the births and deaths of beings, than *without.*"

his own and meditate. He found a cave not too far from a village where he could go on alms rounds and settled in to practice. During the next 20 years, he learned to walk on water—a shortcut to town since there was a river between his cave and the village.

One day he was in town and heard news that his old master was coming for a visit. He excitedly returned home to his cave and made it as nice as he could. And sure enough a few days later his master appeared. They had a joyful reunion. After exchanging many greetings and good wishes, his master said to him, "Well, what have you learned in these 20 years?" The no-longer-so-young man stood up, walked down to the river, and strode across to the other side. He came back all smiles. But his master said to him, "You fool! You've wasted 20 years of your life! There's a bridge a quarter mile upstream."

In the Kevaddha Sutta (DN 11.4 and 7), the Buddha says, referring to both the various supernormal powers and knowing the minds of others, "Seeing the danger of such miracles, I dislike, reject and despise them." There is also a foolish monk named Sunakkhatta who left the monkhood because the Buddha didn't perform any miracles,* which certainly casts doubt on all the accounts of miracles that are found in the suttas.

So don't waste your life messing around with any supernormal powers. The jhānas are for turbocharging your insight practice. Deep insights into the inconstant, ultimately unsatisfactory, empty nature of the universe are what will liberate you from dukkha.

---

* DN 24. Sunakkhatta appears in MN 12 and MN 105 as well. He also complained that the Buddha didn't explain to him the beginning of things.

21 Ending the Āsavas

Concentration, when imbued with ethics, brings great fruit and profit. Wisdom, when imbued with concentration, brings great fruit and profit. The mind imbued with wisdom becomes completely free from the āsavas, that is, from the intoxicants of sensuality, of becoming, of false views and of ignorance. (DN 16.1.12)

THE LAST STEP GIVEN in the gradual training is the ending of the āsavas.* The Pali word *āsava* gets variously translated as "outflows," "influxes," "effluents," "cankers," "taints." According to the Pali Text Society's dictionary, *āsava* literally means "that which flows (out or on to) outflow & influx." It is a word used by the Jains to indicate that which has to be stopped in order to escape the wheel of birth and death—basically, these influxes are the bad karma that has to be avoided. As he so often did, the Buddha took a popular word from a competing spiritual tradition and tweaked it to give it a new meaning. Given that new meaning and the etymological background of *āsava,* it is best translated as "intoxicant"—*in-toxic-ant.* The Pali-English Dictionary gives the following meanings for the word *āsava:*

---

* Bronkhorst (*Two Traditions,* section 7.4, p. 70) states, "The Four Dhyānas and the subsequent destruction of the intoxicants . . . occur very frequently in the canonical scriptures and already made the impression on other investigators of belonging to the oldest layers of the tradition." In a footnote he references articles by Frauwallner, Pande, Schmithausen, Griffiths, and Heiler.

1. spirit, the intoxicating extract or secretion of a tree or flower [think of the opium poppy]
2. discharge from a sore
3. technical term for certain specified ideas which intoxicate the mind (bemuddle it, befoozle it, so that it cannot rise to higher things).

Eric Kolvig gave a very excellent evening dhamma talk in Berkeley, California, back in the mid-1990s in which he said something to the effect that "saṃsāra is not a wheel—it's a drunken party in a casino. Our job is to sober up, find the exit, and get out!" What we are drunk on is the āsavas—we are intoxicated with sense pleasures, we are intoxicated with becoming, and we are intoxicated by ignorance. And in some later suttas, the three āsavas become four with the addition of the intoxicant of views, which of course is just another flavor of ignorance.

What we find as the last step of the gradual training is that after you have concentrated your mind via the fourth jhāna,

> when one's mind is thus concentrated, pure and bright, unblemished, free from defects, malleable, wieldy, steady, and attained to imperturbability, one directs and inclines it to the knowledge of the destruction of the āsavas. One understands as it really is: "This is dukkha." One understands as it really is: "This is the origin of dukkha." One understands as it really is: "This is the cessation of dukkha." One understands as it really is: "This is the way leading to the cessation of dukkha." One understands as it really is: "These are the āsavas." One understands as it really is: "This is the origin of the āsavas." One understands as it really is: "This is the cessation of the āsavas." One understands as it really is: "This is the way leading to the cessation of the āsavas."

> Knowing and seeing thus, one's mind is liberated from the āsava of sensual desire, from the āsava of becoming, and from the āsava of ignorance. (DN 2.99)

The standard formula for the four noble truths—existence, origin, cessation, path—is applied to both dukkha and the āsavas. There is also a simile:

> Suppose in a mountain glen there were a lake with clear water, limpid and unsullied. A man with keen sight, standing on the bank, would see oyster-shells, sand and pebbles, and shoals of fish moving about and keeping still. He would think to himself: "This is a lake with clear water limpid and unsullied, and there within it are oyster-shells, sand and pebbles, and shoals of fish moving about and keeping still." (DN 2.100)

The simile does not seem to be particularly well related to what precedes it. The simile is certainly one of "clear seeing"—insight.[1] It is possible that the formula applied to the truths and to the āsavas has usurped whatever was there originally.[2] But it also could be that what is to be seen is the general applicability of the formula: an item, its arising, its ceasing, and the path leading to its cessation.* The general formula is, of course,

---

* In addition to applying the formula to dukkha and the āsavas, which occurs frequently in all four major Nikāyas, the formula is, for example, also applied to the world in SN 2.26; to the four elements in SN 14.39; to gain, honor, and praise in SN 17.27; to the five aggregates in SN 22, SN 46.30, AN 4.41, and AN 8.2; to feeling in SN 36; to the five faculties in SN 48.7; to the eye faculty and so forth in SN 48.30; to personal existence in AN 4.33; and in AN 6.63 it is applied to sensual pleasures, vedanā, perceptions, āsavas, kamma, and dukkha; in MN 9 it is applied to nutriment, aging and death, birth, becoming, clinging, craving, feeling, sense contact, the sixfold base, mentality-materiality, consciousness, fabrications, and ignorance, as well as to dukkha and the āsavas.

a form of dependent origination. But unmistakably this last step of the gradual training is teaching that if we have clear enough vision, that will enable us to sober up and put an end to the āsavas.*

During the third watch on the night of his awakening, the Buddha attained this third true knowledge—the knowledge of the destruction of the āsavas—which arises when these āsavas are uprooted: "Ignorance was banished and true knowledge arose, darkness was banished and light arose, as happens in one who abides diligent, ardent, and resolute."[3]

Again from the *Pali-English Dictionary:* "Freedom from the 'Āsavas' constitutes Arahantship,† & the fight for the extinction of these āsavas forms one of the main duties of [a human]." On becoming liberated from the āsavas, the gradual training says, "When [your mind] is liberated, the knowledge arises: 'It is liberated.' One understands: 'Birth is destroyed, the holy life has been lived, what had to be done has been done, there is nothing further beyond this.'" The Buddha also called this liberation a visible fruit of the holy life and said, "There is no other fruit of [the holy life] higher or more sublime than this one."[4]

* Bronkhorst (*Two Traditions,* section 8.4.3, 77–79) suggests that the four noble truths are a late insertion since they neither fit in smoothly nor are necessary at this point.

† Full awakening.

22 Other Benefits of Jhāna Practice

The four jhānas that constitute the higher mind and provide a pleasant abiding here and now. (MN 6.9)

ONE OF THE MORE INTERESTING THINGS to come from modern neuroscientific research is the discovery of neural plasticity. This refers to changes in neural pathways and synapses, which are due to changes in behavior, environment, and neural processes, as well as changes resulting from bodily injury.[1] Neuroscientist Richard Davidson writes, "When the framework of neuroplasticity is applied to meditation, we suggest that the mental training of meditation is fundamentally no different than other forms of skill acquisition that can induce plastic changes in the brain."[2] Discussing his work with meditators who are experts in what he calls "focused attention" (FA) he writes:

> The findings support the idea that, after extensive FA meditation training, minimal effort is necessary to sustain attentional focus. Expert meditators also showed less activation than novices in the amygdala during FA meditation in response to emotional sounds. Activation in this affective region correlated negatively with hours of practice in life. This finding may support the idea that advanced levels of concentration are associated with a significant decrease in emotionally reactive behaviors that are incompatible with stability of concentration. Collec-

> tively, these findings support the view that attention is a trainable skill that can be enhanced through the mental practice of FA meditation.[3]

The jhānas are certainly a strong form of FA—focused attention!

The amygdala appears to be the brain structure that is at the very center of most of the brain events associated with fear. Just an eight-week mindfulness meditation program appeared to make measurable changes in brain regions associated with memory, sense of self, empathy, and stress. The study associated with this eight-week program found decreased gray-matter density in the amygdala.[4] This finding, along with less activation in the amygdala during focused attention meditation mentioned above, would indicate that jhāna practice would be expected to have a long-term effect of reducing the automatic fear response.

In his book *Destructive Emotions,* Daniel Goleman discusses research that shows that negative emotional states are correlated with increased activity in the right prefrontal cortex and positive emotional states are correlated with increased activity in the left prefrontal cortex. He also states that the baseline activity of the prefrontal cortex provides an "emotional set point." Furthermore, simply by spending increased amounts of time in positive emotional states and less time in negative emotional states, your emotional set point can be altered toward increased left prefrontal cortex activity—in other words, you can intentionally create a more positive emotional state as your default state.[5] This finding confirms the Buddha's assertion in the Dvedhāvitakka Sutta (MN 19.6) that "whatever one frequently thinks and ponders upon, that will become the inclination of one's mind."

The Buddha spoke of the jhānas as providing a "pleasant abiding here and now"[6]—in other words, since the four jhānas are primarily emotional states, they provide positive emotional abidings. Certainly from a subjective viewpoint, the first three jhānas are positive emotional states. In fact, unmistakable visual evidence provided by fMRI and EEG measurements show that all four jhānas involve increased activity in the left prefrontal cortex—even the subjectively neutral fourth jhāna shows increased left prefrontal cortex activity.[7] Although using the jhānas to move your emotional set point to be more positive is a long-term project—probably involving thousands of hours, it certainly is a nice side effect for a warm-up exercise for gaining insights.

In the Cūḷadukkhakkhandha Sutta (MN 14), the Buddha's cousin Mahānāma the Sakyan says he understands "'greed, hate, delusion [are] imperfections that defile the mind.' Yet while I understand the Dhamma taught by the Blessed One thus, at times states of greed, hate, and delusion invade my mind and remain. I have wondered, venerable sir, what state is still unabandoned by me internally, owing to which at times these states of greed, hate, and delusion invade my mind and remain."

The Buddha replies, "When a noble disciple has seen clearly as it actually is with proper wisdom that sensual pleasures provide little gratification, much suffering and despair, and that the danger in them is still more, and he attains to the rapture and pleasure that are apart from sensual pleasures, apart from unwholesome states, or to something more peaceful than that, then he is no longer attracted to sensual pleasures." In other words, understanding the drawbacks of greed, hate, and delusion is not enough; the experience of rapture and pleasure that are apart from sensual pleasures, apart from unwholesome states, are needed as well. This higher pleasure is available in the first and second jhānas, and the higher jhānas provide "something more peaceful than that." Thus the jhānas serve as an antidote to getting lost in the pursuit of worldly pleasures.

In the Naḷakapāna Sutta (MN 68.6), the Buddha similarly points out how jhāna practice overcomes the five hindrances (including covetousness, often used as a synonym for sensual pleasure), as well as other unwholesome states such as discontent and weariness.

In the second "sermon" in the Mahātaṇhāsaṅkhaya Sutta (MN 38.28-40),* the Buddha teaches the gradual training up through the four jhānas. Post-jhāna, one abandons favoring and opposing, and whatever vedanā one experiences, one does not delight in that vedanā, welcome it, or remain holding to it. Being thus free from craving, one is free from dukkha.

So besides the jhānas being a way to prepare your mind for insight practice, they can also have the following benefits as well:

- reduce effort necessary to sustain attentional focus,
- decrease emotionally reactive behaviors,
- reduce your automatic fear response,
- move your emotional set point in the positive direction,
- provide pleasure more desirable than worldly pleasures, and hence
- provide an antidote to sensual craving,
- provide a pleasant abiding here and now.

---

* MN 38 is composed of two "sermons" on the destruction of craving (taṇhā). The first (MN 38.1–25) is about Sati, who thinks his consciousness transmigrates (an example of bhavataṇhā); there is a "bridge" at MN 38.26–27; and finally there is the second "sermon" on sensual craving (kāmataṇhā).

Afterword

I HOPE YOU HAVE ENJOYED YOUR TOUR through the jhānas as described in the suttas of the Pali canon. These concentration states are skills that are indeed learnable by serious lay practitioners of the buddhadhamma as well as by modern monks and nuns. Facility with the jhānas will certainly enhance your insight practice and perhaps bring a new feeling of excitement to your meditation practice. They also provide a number of positive, long-term side effects as discussed in the previous chapter.

Not everyone who undertakes jhāna practice becomes proficient in these skills, but the only way to find out if they are something that works for you is to try learning them. Just remember: it is certainly much easier to learn the jhānas while on a longer silent meditation retreat. And it helps to have someone with whom you can discuss your experiences as you attempt to enter these states.

There is quite a bit more that can be said about the jhānas. I have included several jhāna-related essays in the following appendices. Hopefully what is there deepens your understanding of these incredibly useful mind states. You can find additional jhāna-related essays at http://rc.leighb.com/more.

Also, please remember: this is just one person's understanding of the jhānas. There are many more interpretations out there. Furthermore, my understanding of the jhānas has changed over time. Had I written this book five years earlier, it would be quite different. Nothing stays the same; everything in the universe is in flux—especially human ideas and understanding. But what is presented here is based on a two-and-a-half-thousand-year-old tradition, and it is both practical and learnable.

May your journey on the spiritual path be of great fruit and great benefit to you and to all beings!

APPENDIX 1: *Frequently Asked Questions*

Do I need exceptional powers of concentration to learn the jhānas?

No. You do need some skill at concentration, but it doesn't have to be exceptional. I have had a number of students in their first interview say to me something like, "I don't know why I'm here on a jhāna retreat—I don't have very good concentration." But yet, an interview or two later they come in and clearly are experiencing one or more jhānas. Remember "concentration" is not the best translation of *samādhi;* much better is "indistractability." Really the only way to find out if you have enough indistractability is to come on a retreat where jhānas are being taught and see what happens. Just be sure to come with no expectations!

I've heard that one can become addicted to the jhānas. Is this true?

It is possible—but certainly it's not something to worry about. In Western civilization, students have their famous short attention span. At first, they get high on the jhānas—it's wonderful! Then they get high—it's wonderful. Then they get high—and it's nice. Then they get high—and it's "been there; done that; what's next?" What's next is insight practice. A skilled jhāna teacher is always carefully checking to see if a student has become overly enamored with the jhānic states and if so, pushes the student to do insight practice in the post-jhānic state of mind. Once the insights start rolling in, the student will have found something far more interesting and rewarding than just getting high. Problem solved.

This is not to say that someone practicing jhānas without the guidance of a competent teacher might not become "addicted" to the jhānic states, although the word *addicted* is quite a stretch since there are absolutely no withdrawal symptoms. But it is true that someone could waste their time just getting superconcentrated and never use their concentrated mind to gain insights. But generally people who do wind up just playing in the jhānas for months or even years on end do begin to wonder, "There's got to be more to this than just getting high!" Hopefully they find someone who can help them channel their concentration skill toward investigating the nature of reality.

Are there people who should not attempt jhāna practice or for whom jhāna practice would be very difficult?

My usual answer to this is that if the jhānas were dangerous, I'd be dead by now. That said, jhāna practice is contraindicated for someone with an untreated tendency toward mania. It seems that frequent, repeated experiences of pīti and/or sukha can lead to an onset of a manic episode. This is thankfully very rare—occurring in less than a tenth of a percent of the over one thousand students I have worked with. Also, as mentioned in chapter 3, "Entering the Jhānas," practice with strong pīti might be contraindicated for someone prone to seizures.

I have had students who were being treated for bipolar disorder and for schizophrenia who had no problems—but their medication left their effect so flat that they were not able to enter a jhāna. So I can say that some psychotropic medications seem to not be compatible with jhāna practice. But of course, for those who need such medication, not taking that medication is not an option either!

I have had a large number of students who were taking medication for depression. They seem to have a slightly more difficult time learning the jhānas, but antidepressants do not seem to be a significant problem.

If the jhānas are so central to the Buddha's teachings, why are they so seldom taught today?

It seems after the Buddha's death, the monks began a slow process of redefining just what constitutes these states. There are hints of this starting to happen in some of the suttas that seem to be very late compositions. See the information about MN 43 and MN 111 mentioned in chapter 12, "First Jhāna." When we look at the jhānas as described in the Abhidhamma, which was composed some one to two hundred or more years after the Buddha's death, what we find being described are states of much deeper absorption. Vitakka and vicāra by that time had been redefined to no longer mean "thinking" but rather "initial and sustained attention on the meditation object," and ekaggata had become an additional factor of the first jhāna. By the time of the *Visuddhimagga,* some eight hundred plus years after the Buddha's death, the jhānas had become redefined to such an extent that it was extremely difficult to learn them. Unfortunately this *Visuddhimagga* description of what constitutes a jhāna persists, for the most part, into the twentieth and twenty-first centuries.

Since the number of people who could actually attain *Visuddhimagga*-style jhānas was quite small, the teaching of jhānas became more and more neglected in favor of "dry insight"—insight meditation without the preliminary jhāna practice. Dry insight practice is doable by almost anyone since it only requires momentary concentration (khaṇika-samādhi).

But even having recovered what the Buddha and his monastics were practicing does not make teaching jhānas an easy task. Students in the West tend to come on short retreats (yes, ten days is quite short when compared to the annual three-month rainy-season retreat for monastics), often bringing expectations—realistic or not, but always hindering the learning of jhānas. Effectively teaching jhānas requires a good bit of one-on-one interview time in addition to providing a clear set of instructions as a starting point. It is quite a lot of work for the teachers and the students, and even students who work very hard are not guaranteed to experience any jhānas.

It's quite a shame that the jhānas have become so neglected. Ayya Khema's teacher, the Venerable Matara Sri Ñanarama Mahathera, after confirming that Ayya was indeed doing the jhānas correctly, added, "And furthermore you must teach them, they are in danger of becoming a lost art."[1]

It says in the suttas that the Buddha-to-be rejected the jhānas he learned from his two teachers.[2] Why would he return to practicing them?

The Buddha-to-be's teachers taught that what we refer to as the seventh and eighth jhānas were the goal of the spiritual path. Master Gotama understood that neither the seventh nor eighth jhāna answered his questions or lead to the end of dukkha, so he left each of his teachers. He then tried austerities practices, but he determined, "By this racking practice of austerities I have not attained any superhuman states, any distinction in knowledge and vision worthy of the noble ones. Could there be another path to awakening?"[3]

He then remembered an incident from his childhood where he had spontaneously entered the first jhāna when seated in the cool shade of a rose apple tree while his father was working. He wondered, "Could that be the path to awakening?" Upon more reflection he decided, "That is indeed the path to awakening."[4] In other words, he realized that the jhānas were part of the path, not the goal. He then used them as a preliminary practice[5] before gaining the insight that led to his awakening and becoming the Buddha.

So he rejected the jhānas as the goal and only later recognized that they were a very useful part of the path to the goal.

What was the reason for this redefinition of jhānas away from how the Buddha understood and practiced them?

We don't really know. My best guess is that the forest monks in the generations after the Buddha's death basically had nothing much to do but sit around and meditate. With this deeply dedicated practice, some of them discovered these deeper states of absorption but failed to recognize them as not being what was talked about in the suttas. However, clearly these deeper states were deemed useful since they became the de facto understanding of the jhānas. These states then needed to be somehow explained by the descriptions given in the suttas. The first of these absorption states certainly had one-pointedness as a quality, so that was added as a "factor" of the first jhāna by simply stating it was implied, even though it is not mentioned in the sutta description. Of course that meant *vitakka* and *vicāra* could no longer mean "thinking" since thinking is incompatible with one-pointedness, so these two words were redefined to mean "initial and sustained attention to the meditation object."

All this has had the unfortunate side effects of not only failing to understand what the Buddha was experiencing and teaching, but also of redefining jhānic concentration to such an extreme depth that almost no one could experience it or use it. The sutta jhānas, which far more people could attain and use, fell into disfavor and were mostly forgotten. This is really a shame since the Buddha's genius in discovering that these states serve wonderfully as a prelude to insight practice was then lost.

Why are no detailed instructions for the jhānas given anywhere in the suttas?

In the preface, I mentioned that the jhānas do not lend themselves to "book learning": they are much more effectively learned one on one with a teacher rather than from only reading (or hearing) instructions. So there would not really be all that much point for the Buddha to go into the details of learning the jhānas in a sutta—which, remember, is a discourse he spoke to an individual or a group. If someone needed to learn the jhānas, it seems quite likely they would be encouraged to study with a teacher who could give them tailor-made instructions as they progressed.

Do the jhānas always arise in 1-2-3-4 order, or can they arise out of order, even skipping some jhānas?

The jhānas do not always arise in order. It's not all that uncommon for someone to generate only mild pīti and therefore not have a really distinct experience of the first jhāna. Now technically, as outlined in the chapter 13, "Second Jhāna," they are actually in the first jhāna with minimum pīti until the thinking subsides and their mind can become unified around the sukha.

Occasionally someone gets no pīti at all but does get strong enough sukha that they are able to go directly into the third jhāna. And it is also not unheard of for someone to wind up going directly into the fourth jhāna. There is no real problem with these as starting points, although it will require more time in whatever is the initial jhāna to let the concentration deepen and really stabilize.

It's also not uncommon that in trying to move from a lower numbered jhāna to the next higher numbered one, someone skips a jhāna. The sequences 1-2-4 and 1-3-4 are not uncommon. It is also not uncommon for someone to go from the fifth jhāna to the seventh when trying to learn the sixth. Much more rare is the sequence 5-6-8, but it does happen.

If someone frequently experienced one of the jhānas other than the first as a child, it is quite common for them to initially enter at that jhāna rather than at the first jhāna. They also seem to be a bit more likely to skip the preceding jhāna when initially trying to learn it and go right into the jhāna they are more familiar with.

In general none of this is a problem. To learn the "missing" jhāna(s)—which is a good idea—it usually works best to go past the missing jhāna and then try to go "up" to the previous numbered jhāna. By spending time in the jhāna after the missing one, you deepen your concentration such that you will have plenty for stabilizing the missing one when you find it. And the transition back to a lower-numbered jhāna is usually quite easy compared to trying to find the next higher-numbered one if you have never experienced it.

When I get really concentrated, my mouth seems to fill up with saliva. What should I do about that?

This is a very commonly reported problem. Normally you swallow automatically whenever you need to without noticing it. But when you get really quiet/concentrated, the act of swallowing becomes this huge thing compared to the ongoing quiet. Therefore, you basically forego swallowing and your mouth fills with saliva. You have two choices—drool or swallow. Swallowing will indeed interrupt your quiet and concentration—but not for very long. Like having to move when a pain becomes too intense, if you decide to swallow, notice the intention to swallow, swallow, and then go right back to what you were doing—it clearly is working. The good news is that this seems to work itself out after about three to six months of concentration practice. When you get skilled in the jhāna, you'll probably find that you swallow as part of moving from one jhāna to the next.

How did your teacher Ayya Khema learn the jhānas?

She taught herself! All she had were the early translations of the suttas from the late 1800s and early 1900s plus a very good translation of the *Visuddhimagga*. She had a very keen mind and always wanted to understand exactly what was happening. I assume, but don't know for sure, that she began stumbling into the early jhānas and, by reading the suttas and the *Visuddhimagga,* figured out that they were jhānas. She would certainly have read all she could find on these states, which would have probably been nothing outside of what is in the suttas and the *Visuddhimagga*.

In her autobiography[6] she mentions sitting in meditation all night during the full moon and deciding she was going to find the immaterial jhānas—and she did. After she had developed some skill in all eight jhānas, she sought a jhāna master who could confirm them. As mentioned above, the Venerable Matara Sri Ñanarama Mahathera confirmed that she was indeed doing the jhānas correctly and had her begin teaching them.

Do the references to pīti and sukha in the 16 steps of mindfulness of breathing[7] refer to the jhānas?

There are certainly those who would argue that steps 5–12 are referring to the jhānas. On the other hand, people who understand the jhānas in terms of what is described in the *Visuddhimagga* would argue that these steps do not refer to the jhānas—this is because their understanding of the jhānas is of states of full absorption, and if you are fully absorbed, there is no way you can be aware of your breathing.

One thing that is quite obvious is that steps 5–12 do involve taking the mind to a deeper level of concentration. But it doesn't really seem likely that these steps refer to the jhānas, at least based on the qualities and the order of the qualities mentioned. In step 5–12, the order of the qualities mentioned is "pīti, sukha, experiencing the mental formation, tranquilizing, experiencing the mind, gladdening (*abhippamodayaṃ*), concentrating and liberating" (MN 118.18). In chapter 16, "The Jhāna Summary," and in the Upanisā Sutta (SN 12.23), the order is gladness (pāmojja), pīti, tranquility, sukha, concentration. Notice that in these latter two obvious jhāna references, gladdening comes first, not after the pīti and sukha. Tranquility comes between pīti and sukha, not after them; liberating the mind isn't even mentioned.

Certainly one could argue that the first 4 steps of mindfulness of breathing can be used to generate access concentration, and the next 8 steps deepen that concentration, while the last 4 steps are clearly insight steps. But it also seems like there are valuable insights to be gained in all 16 steps.

It appears that these 16 steps of mindfulness of breathing are another method for working with concentration and insight that is somewhat different from that described in the gradual training, which includes the jhānas. But there doesn't seem to be enough evidence to settle this discussion, so it will likely continue.

For an excellent detailed exploration of the 16 steps of mindfulness of breathing, please see *Mindfulness with Breathing—A Manual for Serious Beginners* by Ajahn Buddhadasa Bhikkhu (Wisdom Publications, 1996).

Are the last four factors of the seven factors of awakening the same as the jhānas?

The *Seven Factors of Awakening* are

1. mindfulness (sati)
2. investigation of phenomena (dhamma-vicaya)
3. energy (viriya)

4. rapture (pīti)
5. tranquility (passaddhi)
6. concentration (samādhi)
7. equanimity (upekkha)

It certainly is the case that moving through the four jhānas will generate rapture, tranquility, concentration, and equanimity. Although there are teachers who have claimed that the last four factors are identical with the four jhānas, I personally think it is a bit of a stretch. But given that right concentration, the eighth step on the noble eightfold path, is defined as the four jhānas,[8] it certainly seems that in order to perfect the seven factors of awakening, having skill in the four jhānas is going to be extremely helpful. And of course skill in the jhānas generates a mind that can much more easily be mindful and more deeply investigate phenomena.

Are the jhānas necessary for awakening?

It certainly seems that they are not necessary for the first stage of awakening, called *stream-entry*. There are numerous suttas where the Buddha gives a dhamma talk and one or more people experience the first level of awakening. It also appears that many of these people were lay people with no background in meditation—among those who experience stream-entry upon hearing a talk from the Buddha are both a king and a leper. And it seems that even today people experience what seems to be stream-entry without ever practicing the jhānas.

As for whether or not the jhānas are required for full awakening—arahatship—well, you can find plenty of evidence in the suttas to prove that they certainly are required and also that they certainly are not required. I think the only way this question can be decided for full awakening is to do a survey of those who are undoubtedly fully awakened—

but unfortunately people who are unmistakably arahats seem to be in short supply these days.

What is certain is that if you have the necessary concentration skills, the jhānas are definitely helpful on the spiritual path. Equally obvious from the suttas is that the way that the jhānas are most helpful is to use them as a preliminary practice for sharpening your mind prior to doing insight practice—that is, investigate the way things really are with a jhānically enhanced mind.

What are the relationships among the Pali words **samatha** *and* **samādhi, vipassanā** *and* **paññā,** *and jhāna?*

We sometimes hear about "samatha and vipassanā" (e.g., as types of meditation) and about "samādhi and paññā" (e.g., as parts of sīla, samādhi, and paññā). We can define these words as follows:

- samatha—calm
- samādhi—indistractability, concentration
- vipassanā—insight, an understood experience
- paññā—wisdom

Samatha is the Pali word for "calm." Any type of meditation whose primary aim is to generate a calm, collected mind can be referred to as "samatha meditation." All of the methods for generating access concentration discussed in appendix 3 are samatha practices. There are even modern techniques, such as counting sheep to help you fall asleep, which could be referred to as "samatha practice."

When doing any form of samatha meditation, when the mind collects on an object and becomes unlikely to become distracted, then samādhi (indistractability, concentration) has been established. Samādhi is *samatha* par excellence. Samādhi is used to generate the jhānas; then moving through the jhānas will deepen the samādhi.

Once the mind has become concentrated, it can be turned to investigating the nature of reality. This hopefully gives insight (vipassanā) into "things as they really are" in that you have an "understood experience"* of what's actually happening. Wisdom (pañña) arises when the insights are integrated and provide a foundation so that you can operate in harmony with reality.

So first you establish samatha (calm); then deepen that calm until it becomes samādhi (indistractability, concentration). Use this samādhi to generate the jhānas, which will deepen the samādhi. Then upon exiting the jhānas, turn your concentrated mind to investigating the nature of reality so that you can gain insight (vipassanā), which can be integrated to become wisdom (pañña).

How much concentration is required for jhāna?

In Buddhism in the twenty-first century, there is much discussion about the role of jhāna practice in following the Buddha's path. There are those who are quite opposed to any role for the jhānas—though clearly they have not paid careful, open-minded attention to the early teachings in the suttas of the Pali canon. But even among those who feel jhāna practice is important, there is quite a heated discussion as to exactly how much concentration is required for an experience to be classified as a jhāna. Not surprisingly, most jhāna teachers claim that the amount of concentration they teach is the correct amount, and any less concentration is not real jhāna, and any more concentration is simply indulging and a waste of time.

When I was first practicing jhānas, I spoke with a highly respected

* Ayya Khema frequently defined an *insight* as "an understood experience."

teacher in the vipassanā community about my practice. That person gave me truly excellent advice: "We don't really know what the Buddha was practicing, but what you are doing seems to be fine." I had not actually considered that there was any other way than what I was doing; I had just assumed I was doing the one and only correct way since I was gaining so many valuable insights during my insight practice periods using my jhānically concentrated mind.

The question "What was the Buddha's understanding of jhāna practice?" continued to rumble around in my head over the years, especially as I learned that there were a number of competing interpretations of the descriptions of the jhānas found in the suttas. Then in 2006, I had an experience that seemed to shed light on that question. I was attending a month-long retreat with the Venerable Pa Auk Sayadaw at the Insight Meditation Society's Forest Refuge.

The primary access method that Sayadaw teaches is mindfulness of breathing—ānāpānasati. The initial instructions for ānāpānasati from Sayadaw were to learn to follow the breath for half an hour without getting distracted. Since I had been practicing ānāpānasati for over 20 years in one form or another, this was not a difficult thing for me to do. When I reported that I could do so at my next interview, Sayadaw asked me to sit longer—like three or four hours per sitting.

Needless to say, such long sittings quickly built my concentration. And since, for nearly 20 years, I had been using ānāpānasati concentration to access pīti, I began having very strong bursts of pīti. Luckily, these bursts only lasted ten or so seconds—if they had lasted much longer, my head would have probably popped off, the shaking was so strong. I was not doing anything to induce the pīti—it was showing up on its own after I got really concentrated. I reported this to Sayadaw, and he called it "gross pīti" and said it was not helpful and to not do that.

I found that I could prevent the pīti from arising if I was very careful to not smile—I had to keep a very neutral expression on my face—and not get distracted into anything "pleasurable." Yet I could feel the pīti in the background tingling away pretty much all the time; certainly anytime I stopped and looked for it, it was there. But I could prevent the strong outbursts of "gross pīti."

Please note: the following is *not* a description of the jhānas as taught by Venerable Pa Auk—for that see the web page "Visuddhimagga Jhānas" at http://rc.leighb.com/more/Visuddhimagga_Jhanas.htm. These are just my extracurricular explorations. Mostly I concentrated (pun intended) on Sayadaw's ānāpānasati practice. But sometimes after sitting for three or four hours, if I still had energy and my body was willing, I would let the pīti arise (all I had to do was smile for a minute or so) and go off exploring the jhānas as I had learned them from Venerable Ayya Khema.

The pīti would arise and flood my body, and I would experience severe shaking for ten seconds or so. This would calm down, and I would find myself in a state of extreme happiness: sukha. The sukha was huge, and I was intently focused on it. I wouldn't say I was totally absorbed; I could still hear the birds singing outside my window if I turned my mind to them, but I was completely indistractable. My attention was not going anywhere! There was no effort at all involved in being in this state—it was simply my current state of being. So I would sit there with no notion of how long I was staying in the state, just thoroughly enjoying being so happy that I was grinning almost big enough to break my face. From time to time, more bursts of pīti would arise. At first they were as strong and long as the initial burst, but over time they would be less frequent and less intense. I would stay in this state for (I'm guessing) about 15 minutes—with no effort on my part—just sitting and experiencing.

So where was I? Well, this state was certainly familiar from practicing the jhānas as I learned them from Ayya Khema—but far more stable and intense. It's what she called the second jhāna. But what do the suttas say? Well, they describe the first jhāna having four qualities:

- vitakka—thinking
- vicāra—examining
- pīti—glee, rapture
- sukha—happiness/joy

The last two—pīti and sukha—are said to be born of "seclusion" (from the hindrances). Now, the second jhāna arises with the subsiding of the vitakka and the vicāra and also is described as having four qualities:

- sampasādana—inner tranquility (or inner assurance, depending on the translation)
- ekodi-bhavam—unification of mind
- pīti—glee, rapture
- sukha—happiness/joy

The last two—pīti and sukha—are said to be born of "concentration." Well, I certainly was concentrated when I entered this state. And there was no real thinking—I was just there with my calm mind focused in a unified way on the sukha. So I would say I was in the second jhāna—skipping the first because of the strong concentration, which propelled me directly into the second.

As mentioned earlier, in some suttas, the Buddha elaborates that one "drenches, steeps, saturates and suffuses one's body with the pīti and sukha born of concentration so that there is no part of one's body not filled with pīti and sukha" (DN 2.79). Well, there was no action necessary on my part—I was drenched, steeped, saturated, and suffused with the pīti and sukha. It felt like I was immersed in a bowl of sukha; I was completely filled with it, and it totally surrounded me. This wasn't "Oh, I should move the pīti from my chest into my legs"; this was dunked and held under. This experience much more closely matched the sutta description than I'd ever experienced before.

So I'd hang out in this second jhāna for a while and then maybe think to move on to the third jhāna. But it was not within my power to intentionally make that move. I had to wait until the pīti faded away on its own—which could take a while. I'm guessing it was over a 15-minute span from the time of the initial burst of strong pīti until it faded away and didn't return. At that time, the sukha would calm down and the "break-your-face grin" would become more of a nice grin. And everything would become very unmoving, very still. I was now in a calmer, steadier, and still quite happy place—the third jhāna, I presume. There was still no need to intentionally focus on the sukha—it just was there, and my attention was riveted on it.

Eventually, the happiness would fade out, and I'd be in a very nice neutral state of mind—very calm, very still. And my visual field would go all white. This state would only last a minute or so; then a sinking feeling would appear. I would just go with the feeling of sinking down, down, down. Eventually the sinking would stop, and I'd be in what I would say was the fourth jhāna. The energy level had certainly decreased, but I did not experience the pronounced slumping I often encounter in the fourth jhāna when I enter it with less concentration; I sagged slightly rather than slumped.

My visual field remained white during this sinking and settling phase. The description of the fourth jhāna sometimes adds, "One sits suffusing one's body with a clear, bright mind" (DN 2.83). Definitely my visual field was bright white, and that brightness seems to extend to the non-visual aspects of my experience—there was a brightness and clarity to the whole experience.

The simile given for the fourth jhāna is a "man covered from the head down by a white cloth" (DN 2.84). This fourth-jhāna experience was like sitting outside on a bright sunny day with a white sheet thrown over me—except there was no sense of touch, and my eyes were closed. But everything seemed close in and bright white. For the first time, I had a deep appreciation of how extremely accurate the simile for the fourth jhāna actually is—it really captures the experience.

As mentioned in chapter 7 on the fourth jhāna, at the time of the Buddha, after the monks and nuns finished their alms rounds, they would eat their midday meal, which would be at around ten or eleven o'clock in the morning. Then they would "go for the day's abiding"[9] and meditate until evening. Since they had not grown up with chairs, they had the capacity to sit cross-legged for an extended period of time. So if they were sitting for multiple hours at a time over a six- or seven-hour period, they were far more likely to experience a very deep level of concentration. By the time they entered the fourth jhāna, their concentration was deep enough that the simile with its white cloth indeed captured the pure, bright mind they were experiencing.

So it turns out we do have enough information in the suttas to set minimum and maximum bounds on how much concentration the composers of the suttas* were experiencing in their jhāna practice. The maximum strength would be limited by the phrase "One drenches, steeps, saturates, and suffuses one's body." Clearly in the first four jhānas, there cannot be such a strong a level of concentration that you lose touch with your body. Thus in the suttas, the jhānas cannot be full absorption since in full absorption there is no body awareness at all.

The minimum strength of concentration for the composers of the

---

*The usual assumption that the suttas accurately reflect what the Buddha and his monks and nuns were practicing is just that—an assumption.

suttas would be that concentration has to be strong enough concentration to generate the pure bright mind with its bright white visual field in the fourth jhāna.

So if we want to have a strictly sutta-based answer to the question "How much concentration is required for jhāna?" the answer would be at least enough to generate the pure bright mind of the fourth jhāna and not so much as to lose touch with your body. This information gets us about as close as we can get to answering the question "What was the Buddha's understanding of the jhānas?"

But remember: the Buddha was an incredibly practical teacher. I think he would agree that any amount of concentration that managed to enhance your investigation of reality would be better than no additional concentration. So whether or not you can spend the hours in access concentration sufficient to generate the bright white visual field and the pure bright mind of the fourth jhāna, generate whatever concentration you can as a prelude to your insight practice!

As mentioned earlier, I have been accused of teaching "Jhāna Lite." Well, certainly what I teach is "lite" compared to what is described in the *Visuddhimagga*—but the depth of concentration described there, since it involves full absorption in even the first jhāna, does exceed the upper bound of what is taught in the suttas. But what I teach would be considered "lite" compared even to the sutta description. However, what I teach is what a lay person can learn in a ten-day retreat. And if they learn it well and apply it as a warm-up for their insight practice, they will benefit greatly from even that level of increased concentration. And if they want to further increase the depth of concentration experienced in the jhānas, then all that is necessary is to increase the amount of time spent in access concentration.

Really the question "How much concentration is required for jhāna?" is not the best question to ask. The real question is "How much concentration can I generate as a prelude to my insight practice given the constraints of my life?" It's much better to generate a so-called lite version of the jhānas than to throw up your hands and not enhance your concentration at all because of not being able to experience some deeper idealized version. The methods described in this book do teach a way to enhanced concentration that is accessible and highly beneficial when applied to "seeing things as they really are."

APPENDIX 2:

Helpful Things to Do at the Beginning and End of Each Meditation Period

THERE ARE FIVE THINGS YOU CAN DO at the beginning of a meditation period that will help you get settled and will prepare your mind for meditation. There are also five additional things you can do at the end of a meditation period that will help consolidate the gains you have made during that period.

Five Things to Do at the Beginning of Meditation

It is very helpful after you get seated in your comfortable, upright posture to generate some *gratitude*—gratitude toward your teachers who have taught you the dhamma, gratitude for the life circumstance that enables you to undertake this period of meditation practice, gratitude for all the millions of people who have had a hand in preserving the Buddha's dhamma for two and half thousand years, gratitude to the Buddha for finding and showing the way, gratitude for anything else that you are currently grateful for. This begins to settle your mind into a positive state, which will be helpful for entering the jhānas. Also current neuroscience research has shown that gratitude practice begins the process of shutting down the so-called default-mode network, which is responsible for many of our distractions.

A second preliminary is to get in touch with your *motivation.* Why are you doing this practice? Whatever it is, getting it clear in your mind hopefully will inspire you. Then work up some *determination*—not determination to get anything, just determination to do your very best to use this time as wisely as possible. Get as strong a sense of that as you can; then let it go. It is not useful to begin your practice with a tight mind. But a few moments of working up some determination will have a residual effect that will carry over into your access meditation, when you begin that.

At the beginning of every meditation period, you should always do some *mettā* (loving-kindness) practice—always for yourself, and additionally for others, if you wish. Mettā practice enhances the positive mind state generated moments earlier by the gratitude practice, as well as starting to generate some concentration. If mettā meditation is not something you like doing, it is still required that you do at least a little at the beginning of every sitting. You don't have to feel anything; you just have to remind yourself that it really is OK to be well and happy, and that it would be nice if others that you know are also well and happy. Don't feel you have to do this mettā practice for an extended period—30 seconds is fine. And don't feel you have to send mettā to everyone you know—the nice people and the difficult people. It's OK to just do mettā for yourself (always required!) and for a few people you really like. Of course doing more than 30 seconds of mettā and sending it to more individuals and various groups, including "all living beings everywhere," is also fine; it's just not required as part of this preliminary. For more information on mettā practice, see appendix 3, "Access Concentration Methods."

The last of the five things to do at the start of a meditation period is only useful if you are using mindfulness of breathing as your access method; otherwise, just skip it. There is a gatha (saying) from Thich

Nhat Hanh: "Breathing in, I calm body and mind. Breathing out, I smile."[1] This is exactly what you need to do to generate access concentration using mindfulness of breathing. Don't take the saying too literally—just breathe in and out and smile and get calm.

Five Things to Do at the End of Meditation

The five things to do at the end of a meditation period begin with *recapitulation*—what did you do, and how did you get there? This includes remembering what your posture was at the beginning of the period, what it was like to do the five preliminaries mentioned above, what you used for your access method, how you knew you were in access, how long you stayed in access, what was the pleasant sensation that you switched to, what was it like to be with that pleasant sensation, how did the jhāna begin to manifest (if one did), how you responded, and so forth. In fact it can be helpful to remember things that you did before coming to meditate: Had you just eaten? Had you just come back from a walk? Did you read something inspiring?

If you have a meditation the likes of which you would like to have again, it is helpful to know the factors that went into generating that experience. So remember anything that might be relevant. Then when you meditate the next time, try, to the best of your ability, to repeat those factors. You are not going to be able to repeat the experience—that's over and gone. But you will have a better chance of having new experiences similar to the previous one if you have some idea of what you did to generate that previous experience. Not everything you remember preceding some meditation experience is going to be relevant—just keep doing the recapitulation after each sitting, and eventually you'll discover the important contributing factors. This recapitulation is also useful if you have a meditation session the likes of which you never want to have again—remember all the things that happened prior to and during that session, and see if you can figure out which one(s) might have been detrimental.

The second thing to do at the end of a sitting is reflect on *impermanence*—all those high, but mundane, concentration states are now gone; they too are impermanent. The Buddha said, "It is better to live a single day perceiving how things rise and fall than to live a century not perceiving this."[2] The jhānas are impermanent, just like all the other things of saṃsāra. Directly experiencing this is insight into impermanence, one of the three "marks of existence," which constitute the primary areas of exploration that lead to liberating insight.

The third reflection is *insight:* Did you get any insights? What were they? Insights are understood experiences. Some insights are personal; the deepest ones are about the impermanent, ultimately unsatisfying, empty nature of the universe. If you gained any insight, it is very helpful to keep bringing it to mind. Insights really only have a transformative capacity if you can keep them fresh in your memory. Remembering them, if you gained any, at the end of a sitting is the way to begin to keep them fresh. Otherwise they seem to slink back there with your long-forgotten high school foreign language and don't resurface until you have another experience that reminds you, "Oh, yes, I knew that—but I forgot."

The meditation practice you do has effects beyond just you personally. Recognizing this is quite helpful and a good way to remember it is to *dedicate the merit* from this sitting for the liberation of all beings. You can just think something like, "May the merit from this meditation period be for the liberation of all beings everywhere." This helps to counteract any selfishness ("What a great meditator I am!") and puts you in touch with the fact that we all are interrelated and in this together.

The chapter on the preliminaries mentioned that unrelenting *mindfulness* was an extremely important practice to undertake while learning the jhānas. Therefore, just before you get up from your seat, resolve to be mindful as you arise and go about your activities. Continuous mindfulness is very difficult—you need all the help you can get. So make it a habit to remind yourself to be mindful as the last thing at the end of every period of formal meditation.

All of these are just suggestions. If you already have nice preliminary and postmeditation routines, feel free to stick with them, or modify them with any of the above suggestions that seem useful. It really does help to have a way to get settled before starting to meditate, and it certainly helps to do whatever you can to consolidate any gains you've made during a meditation period.

APPENDIX 3:
Access Concentration Methods

THE *Visuddhimagga* mentions thirty different meditation methods for generating access concentration.[1] Most any practice that generates a calm (samatha) mind can be used to generate access concentration. Below, several access methods are described in some detail.

Mindfulness of Breathing

Probably the most frequently used method of generating access concentration is the practice known as *ānāpānasati.** The first word, *ānāpāna,* means "in-breath and out-breath," and the word *sati* means "mindfulness." The practice is therefore "mindfulness of breathing."

The description of mindfulness of breathing begins, "One sits down crossed legged, holds one's body erect and sets up mindfulness before oneself."[2] Sitting cross-legged was a lot easier in the time of the Buddha because people didn't often have chairs, so they habitually sat cross-legged on a mat or the floor. Many of us have lost that ability, so it's perfectly OK to kneel on a bench or sit in a chair. What you want to do

* This description of ānāpānasati is for the sake of access concentration and then jhāna. For a full treatment of ānāpānasati as a complete system of mindfulness training and samatha-vipassanā, please see MN 118 and Buddhadasa Bhikkhu's excellent book *Mindfulness with Breathing.*

is to be able to put your body in a position where you can just leave it relatively comfortable for the length of the meditation period. If it's too uncomfortable, you'll have aversion in your mind, which is an unwholesome state that will keep you out of the jhāna.

You want to sit upright, especially if you are doing mindfulness of breathing. The upright posture helps keep you awake, and it also makes the breathing happen more easily, and therefore it is easier to be mindful of it. After you have settled in, put your attention on the physical sensations associated with your breathing. Pay attention to your breath at your nostrils if you can. Paying attention at the nostrils is more difficult than at the belly or the chest—you have to concentrate more because it's a more subtle object. If you can successfully concentrate on the breath at the nostrils, you have more concentration than if you successfully concentrate on the breath at the belly. Since you need a strong level of concentration to enter the jhāna, it's helpful to work with the more subtle object of the breath at the nostrils.

The phrase *parimukhaṃ satiṃ upaṭṭhapetvā,* often translated as "one sets up mindfulness before oneself," would literally be translated as "one sets up mindfulness at the mouth/entrance." The word *mukha* means "mouth" or "entrance"—think of the mouth of a cave. This would mean at the entrance of the nostrils if breathing through your nose, or at the lips if breathing through your mouth (e.g., if you had a cold). This has later been interpreted to mean either at the nostrils or on the area between the nose and the upper lip. If you are going to pay attention at the nostrils, it can be done right at the opening or just a little bit inside—but don't try to go in too deep; stay near the entrance. But it's really just where you feel the breath. You are to notice the tactile sensations associated with breathing: the coolness as the air comes in, the warmth as it goes out, or however you experience it.

If you have been paying attention to the rise and fall of the belly or the chest for many years, you may find it very difficult to change to paying attention at the nostrils. Just try it and see what it's like—see if you can make the switch. If indeed you can make the switch, it's actually going to be very useful because when you put your attention at the nostrils, you're signaling yourself, "concentrate"; when you put your breath at the belly or chest, you're signaling yourself, "do insight practice," and that can be quite useful. If you find that trying to make the switch is too problematic, go back to whatever you're used to, but be patient before doing so. It is probably going to take working with the breath at the nostrils on a silent retreat at least for a full day—or more—to learn what it's like and successfully make the switch.

There are some aids that you can use that can be very helpful when you are trying to get settled. They won't take you all the way to access concentration, but when you first sit down to meditate, you might find that your mind is all over the place. To help you overcome these initial distractions, you can try one of these aids.

The first aid is counting. Traditionally you count one on the in-breath, one on the out-breath; two on the in-breath, two on the out-breath; up to ten. If you get to ten, go back to one. If you get lost, go back to one. That will work, but an even more effective way of counting is to count the gap between the out-breath and the next in-breath. You breathe in, you breathe out—one. Breathe in, breathe out—two. Think of tossing the number in the gap. Most people find they are more likely to get lost on the out-breath. The air goes out and so do you. If you are really going to be fully present to toss the number right in that gap, you've got to be paying careful attention. And you should count only up to eight. It's easy to go on automatic from one to ten and then back to one. Eight is an unaccustomed stopping place; thus you have to pay more careful attention. So count only up to eight. If you get to eight, go back to one. If you get lost, go back to one. There are no prizes for getting to eight. If you get lost, it's no big deal. If you're not sure, just go back to one—it doesn't matter. You want to make sure to get the number in the gap, not at the end of the out-breath. You'll find that as you begin to lose your focus, you'll start counting the end of the out-breath, rather than the gap. If you notice that, it's no big deal; just pay more careful attention and toss the next number in the gap.

The second possible aid is helpful if you are very visual. You can visualize an ocean wave coming in on the in-breath and then going out on the out-breath. Another wave coming in on the next in-breath, going out on the out-breath. Some people find this works to quiet the distractions for them.

A third aid is to use a word or a pair of words. If you use a single word, it should have two syllables, like the traditional *buddho.* So think "bud" on the in-breath, "dho" on the out-breath: "bud," "dho," "bud," "dho." Another possibility is to use two one-syllable words. You could breathe in "peace" and breath out "love"—"peace," "love." It doesn't matter what word or words you use; just use whatever seems appropriate to you.

The fourth possibility is to look at the details of the breath. Can you pick out the beginning of the in-breath, middle of the in-breath, end of the in-breath, the gap, the beginning of the out-breath, middle of the out-breath, end of the out-breath, the gap? Don't try to name all these parts; it goes far to fast for that. Just notice them.

The fifth aid is the one from the suttas where mindfulness of breathing is discussed.[3] That aid is to notice the long breaths and the short breaths. Pay attention to each in-breath and notice if the current one is longer than average or shorter than average. Do the same for each out-breath. You can also pay attention to see if every long in-breath is always followed by a long out-breath—and the same for short in- and out-breaths.

These are the possible aids: counting the gaps between the out- and the in-breaths up to eight; a visualization, like an ocean wave; a word or pair of words, like "bud-dho" or "peace" and "love"; noticing the details—beginning, middle, end, gap, beginning, middle, end, gap—and noticing the relative lengths of each in- and out-breath. They can help get you to the point where you're not becoming distracted. But this is not yet access concentration. Let go of the aid—stop the counting, stop the visualization, stop the word, stop really looking at the parts of the breath, stop working to notice the lengths of the breaths—and just be with the breath. When you do, it's going to feel like you have regressed because you'll likely start becoming distracted again. It's OK; just keep relaxing and coming back to the breath, and eventually you'll settle in again, knowing each and every in-breath and out-breath. When you are knowing every in-breath and out-breath, and you're not getting distracted and you're not using an aid, that's access concentration.

In summary, sit in a comfortable, upright posture that you can maintain for the length of the sitting. Put your attention on the breathing by noticing the tactile sensations associated with it. Pay attention at the nostrils if possible, or the belly or the chest. You can use one of the aids. When you get distracted, which is no big deal, label the distraction and then intentionally relax. Bring your attention back to the tactile sensations of breathing. Repeat until you feel settled. If you're still using an aid, drop the aid; repeat until you feel settled without the aid; then you're at access concentration. Then stay at access concentration for 5, 10, 15 minutes, if you want to enter the jhānas.

The following questions on mindfulness of breathing as an access method arose after I had presented the above material on a retreat:

QUESTION: I guess I don't think of noticing the parts of the breath as being a technique or an aid. If one drops that, isn't one still noticing all the parts and pieces of the in-breath and the out-breath?

ANSWER: There's still noticing of the whole breath cycle but not an attempt to notice "that's the beginning," "that's the middle," "that's the end." So it's like you're noticing the breath more holistically, and you're no longer trying to divide it into the pieces. Does that make sense?

QUESTION: I guess it's a question of degree then?
ANSWER: If you have a clipboard with papers attached, you know this is the clip part, and this is the paper, and here's the front, and here's the back, and there is writing on the paper. It's like you're almost straining to see the bits and pieces. When you drop the aid, it's like you are seeing just the clipboard, not the individual pieces that make up the clipboard.

QUESTION: And when you're using this as an aid, it's a constant, dedicated effort?
ANSWER: Yes, dedicating effort to recognize, "that's the beginning of the in-breath," "ah, that's the middle of it," "this is the end of it." You can't be mentally saying all that; it's just really working to know all the individual pieces. Whereas when you are settled and drop the aid, there's just the breathing. All those pieces are still there—none of them are unnoticed—but your awareness becomes more holistic, rather than focused on the parts.

Mettā Meditation

Loving-kindness meditation—mettā meditation—can be used very effectively to generate access concentration and enter the jhānas. There are a number of ways to do mettā meditation, and all of them will work as long as you really are seriously doing the mettā practice and not thinking about where you hope it will take you.

All the methods of mettā meditation involve wishing that you and others be well and happy. This is generally done by working with categories. The first category is yourself. You really do want to experience well-being—regardless of whether or not you have any hang-ups about deserving well-being. Forget about deserving happiness, "deserving" is not ever part of mettā practice: not part of it when you are directing mettā to yourself and not part of it when you are directing it to anyone else. Although mettā is usually translated as "loving-kindness," it really is "unconditional love." "Deserving" has no part in something unconditional. The far enemy—the opposite—of mettā is hatred; this is obvious. The near enemy—something that masquerades as mettā—is said to be attachment. But we could also say the near enemy of mettā is "conditional liking." So true mettā practice is simply wishing the best for someone just because they are a someone.

When you are using mettā as an access method, begin your mettā practice with at least five minutes of wishing yourself well. Then move on to the other categories of beings. You can pick one individual per category, or you can think of multiple beings in each category. You want to spend at least half an hour practicing mettā to generate access concentration, so don't rush. The usual categories recommended for mettā practice can be summarized as follows:

- yourself
- people you admire—your benefactors for example
- people you are close to—your family and friends
- neutral people—your acquaintances, such as neighbors, coworkers, people you see in stores and restaurants you frequent
- difficult people—ones who have harmed you or those you care about or who have caused harm to society or the environment
- all beings—you can start with those in your physical proximity and work outward in expanding areas until you cover the whole planet; then expand your mettā to all the beings in the entire universe

If you have trouble sending mettā to yourself, then it's a very good idea to come back to yourself at the end of any period of mettā meditation and once again spend some time wishing yourself well.

The most commonly taught method of mettā meditation is done by silently repeating phrases. It is best to have about four simple phrases. Complicated phrases and more than four of them don't as easily generate the concentration necessary. I suggest using something like the following:

May (I/you/all beings) be happy.
May (I/you/all beings) be healthy.
May (I/you/all beings) be safe.
May (I/you/all beings) be at peace.

Just be sure to pick words that you resonate with.

You may find that it is difficult to wish happiness, health, and safety to the difficult people. If that's the case, you might want to try the phrases that Ayya Khema suggested, which are more closely related to what is found in the suttas:

May (I/you/all beings) be free from enmity.
May (I/you/all beings) be free from hurtfulness.
May (I/you/all beings) be free of troubles of mind and body.
May (I/you/all beings) be able to protect (my own/your/their) happiness.

You certainly can wish difficult people be free of hostility and hurtfulness. You can wish that they be free of troubles of mind—after all, then they would not be so difficult. Maybe their difficulty stems in part from troubles of body, so maybe you can wish they be free of bodily troubles as well. And when you understand that the only happiness that can be protected is that which is generated via wise and wholesome actions, you can even wish difficult people have happiness that can be protected.

The purpose of the phrases is to help you generate the feeling. Once the feeling of mettā becomes strong, it is not necessary to always say the entire phrase. You might then switch to just saying the key words: *happy, healthy, safe, peace.* And the time between the words might grow longer as the feeling grows stronger. Use the phrases or words just enough to keep the mettā feeling strong.

A second way of doing mettā meditation is by using a visualization. Ayya Khema had dozens of these visualizations[4] that she would choose from for her guided mettā meditation each evening. The following is one of these visualizations:

> Please put the attention on the breath for just a few moments.
>
> Imagine that your heart is filled with sunshine. Feel the warmth of it. The brightness. The satisfaction that it brings. The contentment. Let that sun in your heart fill you with joy and embrace you.
>
> Now let the sun in your heart shine on the person nearest you in this room. Bringing with it the love and joy that your heart contains, filling him or her with these feelings as your gift.
>
> And now let the sun from your heart expand so that it can shine on everyone here, bringing with it the best that your heart has to offer. Warmth. Love. Peace. Joy.
>
> Let the sun in your heart shine on your parents, bringing them the warmth, the fulfillment, the joy and the peace that your heart contains.
>
> Let the sun in your heart shine on those people who are nearest and dearest to you, giving them the best that your heart has

to offer. Brightness. Warmth. Love. Fill them with those feelings. Embrace them with the sunshine from your heart.

Think of your friends. Let the sun from your heart shine on each one of them, filling their hearts with the warmth of sunshine, the feeling of joy, being embraced by the rays of the sun. Feeling loved and protected.

Think of other people you know, whomever they might be. Let the sun from your heart expand so that the rays can warm these people, bringing them joy and love.

Think of anyone whom you might have difficulties with. The sun shines indiscriminately on everyone. Let the sun from your heart shine on that person with the warmth and the joy and the love that the sun entails, because it makes everything grow.

Open your heart as wide as you can. Let the sun in your heart shine on as many people as you can imagine, bringing the warmth and the care from your heart to them. Filling them with joy, surrounding them with love.

Put your attention back on yourself. Feel the warmth of the sun in your heart. Feel the joy of sharing and the peacefulness of a loving heart. Fill yourself with that joy. Embrace yourself and surround yourself with peace, feeling safe and protected in that embrace.

May there be sunshine in everyone's heart.

Of course you can run through the above in less than a minute, but that won't generate access concentration. If you are using a visualization like the above, you should spend a number of minutes with each category so that the whole practice takes half an hour or more.

If you can just generate the feeling of love without using any words or any visualization, that works fine as well for generating access concentration. Again, start with yourself and move on to the other categories, taking at least half an hour. You might find it helpful to say a word or two from the phrases if the mettā feeling starts to fade. It's analogous to a potter kicking the flywheel to impart more momentum. The potter doesn't kick continuously—only as needed.

No matter what method you choose for doing mettā meditation, you have to do it whole-heartedly. A thought of the jhānas should not cross your mind while doing the half hour or more of mettā practice. You also don't need to wonder if your practice is having an effect on the other person—that doesn't really matter. It is definitely having an effect on you, and that effect will carry over to the next time you encounter that person.

Unlike the breath becoming very subtle, there is no really obvious marker of access concentration when using mettā as the access method. It is possible the diffused white light might appear, but it seems to do so less frequently when doing mettā than when doing mindfulness of breathing. Your best markers of whether or not you have reached access concentration are twofold: you are continually with the mettā feeling, not getting distracted, and it seems like at least half an hour has passed. Then drop your attention to the feeling of mettā and of those to whom you are sending it, and switch your attention to a pleasant physical sensation. Most likely you will find such a sensation in the area of your heart. Just lock your attention onto that feeling, enjoy it fully, and let the jhāna come find you.

It is possible to remain focused on just the mettā feeling itself as the pleasant sensation. If you wish to go that route, it is necessary that the feeling remain strong without using any word or phrase or visualization. Whether the pleasant sensation is physical or mental, just fix your attention onto it and enjoy it without distraction.

If you find your mind wandering away from the pleasant feeling too much, you might not have generated access concentration. You can at that point go back to doing more mettā and try again later, or switch to mindfulness of breathing. If you choose to switch to your breathing, follow the instructions given in chapter 3, "Entering the Jhānas." If the pleasant feeling disappears, then you will have to either go back to doing mettā practice or switch to mindfulness of breathing.

If either of these happens, during the next meditation period that you attempt to use mettā to generate access concentration, be sure to stay longer with the mettā practice before switching to the pleasant feeling. If the problem persists over many meditation periods, it may be necessary to go from mettā practice directly to the breath, let concentration deepen there, and then switch to the pleasant feeling.

For people who really like doing mettā meditation, this is a very effective way to generate access concentration and enter the jhānas. Not only are you becoming concentrated, you are generating a very positive state of mind, which is very helpful in getting the sukha going. In fact, it is not uncommon for someone who is using mettā as their access method to get mostly sukha and very little pīti when the jhāna arrives. Don't worry about that—just put your attention on the sukha feeling, stay locked onto it, and let your mind absorb into it to such an extent that any background thinking subsides. Then you arrive in the second jhāna without experiencing an overly excited, gleeful first jhāna.

The relationship between mettā meditation and the jhānas that is found in the suttas is reversed from what is described above. Mettā is not used to generate access concentration, but rather in the Tevijja Sutta (DN 13), the first jhāna is used as a preliminary practice before beginning mettā meditation and the other three brahma-vihāras meditations. In that sutta the usual gradual training steps of precepts, guarding the senses, mindfulness, contentment, and abandoning the five hindrances are followed by only the first jhāna. "Then with one's heart filled with loving-kindness, one dwells suffusing one quarter, the second, the third, the fourth. Thus one dwells suffusing the whole world, upwards, downwards, across, everywhere, always with a heart filled with loving-kindness, abundant, unbounded, without hate or ill-will" (DN 13.76). The vitakka and vicāra of the first jhāna are intentionally directed to "thinking"* the mettā practice, with the pīti and sukha remaining low-grade and in the background. The three additional brahma-vihāra practices of compassion, appreciative joy, and equanimity can be done in turn, following time spent doing the mettā practice. This is a wonderful way to do brahma-vihāra practices, but it turns out to be very important to keep the pīti at a very low level—pīti that is too strong tends to generate unwanted distractions.

In the mythological Mahāsudassana Sutta (DN 17), all four jhānas are practiced before beginning the same fourfold brahma-vihāra practice.[5]

Body Scan, also Known as Sweeping

S. N. Goenka made this technique well known in the West, although his teacher U Ba Khin deserves a great deal of credit as well. There are a number of ways to do a body scan, but the most effective way for generating access concentration seems to be to sweep your attention systematically over every square inch of the surface of your body, noticing whatever sensation you can along the way. Don't worry if you encounter places where there are no sensations—zero is a valid number. The scan should be done slowly and take about 35 to 40 minutes. Even if a

---

* Pali, like many Asian languages, does not distinguish between thoughts and emotions. Hence "thinking" would be the word used for "feeling" mettā and the other three brahma-vihāras emotions.

pleasant sensation is encountered or arises somewhere else in your body, complete the scan of your whole body before switching to focusing on the pleasant sensation. You want to let the concentration become sufficiently strong so that you can stay with the subtle pleasant sensation until the jhāna arises. If there is not a pleasant sensation noticeable when you finish the body scan, switch your attention to following your breathing, and continue with the instructions in the chapter "Entering the Jhānas."

If you want to learn how to do this method, it is very helpful to have someone guide you through the scan at least once and maybe even several times. There are MP3s of Ayya Khema doing a guided body scan, which she refers to as "part-by-part," at http://dharmaseed.org/teacher/334/talk/8001/19960705-Ayya_Khema-GGZ-guided_sweeping_meditation_part_by_part.mp3 and http://dharmaseed.org/teacher/334/talk/7819/19950706-Ayya_Khema-NTG-sweeping_technique_part_by_part.mp3. There is an MP3 of me doing a guided body scan at http://www.audiodharma.org/mp3files/2007-02-03_LeighBrasington_GuidedMeditationBodySweep.mp3.

Nada Sound, also Known as the Sound of Silence

Students of Ajahn Sumedho and the other monastics from Amaravati Buddhist Monastery in England may be familiar with working with the "nada sound," or "sound of silence." Ajahn Sumedho talks at length about this technique in his books *The Way It Is* and *Sound of Silence.* Ajahn Amaro, one of Ajahn Sumedho's students, writes

> Nada is the Sanskrit word for "sound," and nada yoga means meditating on the inner sound, also referred to as the sound of silence. (Interestingly, nada is also the Spanish word for "nothing.")
>
> To detect the nada sound, turn your attention toward your hearing. If you listen carefully to the sounds around you, you're likely to hear a continuous, high-pitched inner sound like white

> noise in the background. It is a sound that is beginningless and endless.
>
> There's no need to theorize about this inner vibration in an effort to figure out exactly what it might be. Just turn your attention to it. If you're able to hear this inner sound, you can use the simple act of listening to it as another form of meditation practice, in the same way one uses the breath as an object of awareness. Just bring your attention to the inner sound and allow it to fill the whole sphere of your awareness.[6]

Following the above simple instructions will generate nice, deep access concentration—in people who like listening to this inner sound. Others find the sounds annoying or worry about training themselves to always hear this sound; this practice is not useful for them. But if you like working in this way, listen to this sound of silence for about half an hour. If at that point you are no longer becoming distracted, drop your attention from that sound, and focus your attention on a pleasant sensation. Stay focused on the pleasantness of that pleasant sensation, enjoy it, and let the jhāna come and find you.

Again there are no distinct markers to tell you when you have generated access concentration, other than perhaps the diffused white light might appear. It's best to use the fact that you are not getting distracted, and it seems like at least half an hour has passed.

Mantra

Although the word *mantra* is almost never mentioned in vipassanā or Theravadan Buddhism,* mantras are a highly effective way of getting

---

* Ajahn Sao, Ajahn Mun, Ajahn Chah, Ajahn Thate, Ajahn Maha Bua, and Ajahn Lee all taught using "bud-dho" when breathing in and out. This is mantra meditation in the Thai Forest Tradition—see Polak, *Reexamining Jhāna,* 181.

deeply concentrated. In fact, that is exactly why mantra meditation was developed. It is far beyond the scope of this book to discuss how to do mantra meditation, but if you already know a form of mantra meditation, you can use it to generate access concentration. A shorter mantra is usually better than a lengthy one for generating concentration.

As with all access methods, after having done your preliminaries as described in appendix 2, "Helpful Things to Do at the Beginning and End of Each Meditation Period," begin saying your mantra silently. Eventually instead of it feeling like you are doing the mantra, it will feel as though the mantra is doing you. Now you are likely to have arrived at access concentration—provided of course that you are not becoming distracted. Stay with the mantra doing you for five to ten minutes; then drop the mantra, and switch your attention to a pleasant sensation. As usual, stay focused on the pleasantness of that pleasant sensation, enjoy it, and let the jhāna come and find you.

Other Methods

As mentioned above, the *Visuddhimagga* gives quite a number of additional methods for generating access concentration. Most prominent is meditation on a kasiṇa—a color disk about the size of a dinner plate. The *Visuddhimagga* goes into a quite detailed description of how this is done,[7] along with discussing other techniques as well.[8] Just remember that the jhānas being discussed in the *Visuddhimagga* are not the same as what is found in the suttas; the *Visuddhimagga* jhānas require far more concentration. However, the techniques described there are nonetheless useful for learning the other access methods not described in this book.

APPENDIX 4:

In or Out: The Relationship between Jhāna Practice and Insight Practice

ONE OF THE ONGOING DEBATES among jhāna practitioners is the relationship between the jhānas and insight practice. In one camp are those who think insight practice should be done while remaining in the jhānas. In the other camp are those who say that insight practice needs to be done upon emerging from the jhānas.

Those who feel insight practice should be done while in the jhānas usually cite the Anupada Sutta at MN 111. But as can be seen on the web page "MN 111" at http://rc.leighb.com/more/MN_111.htm, MN 111 is not a reliable source of information as to what the Buddha was teaching. Another possible source of inspiration for suggesting that insight practice be done while in the jhānas could be the Mahāmāluṅkya Sutta at MN 64. But again this sutta is not a reliable source, as it appears to be a relatively late composition.[1]

Those who feel insight practice is best done after the jhānas point to the gradual training, particularly to the insight step found after the description of the fourth jhāna.[2] Their argument is that vitakka and vicāra ("thinking and examining," or "thinking and more thinking") has subsided by the time one enters the second jhāna. Without vitakka and vicāra, it is not possible to understand "This is my body, having material form, composed of the four primary elements, originating from mother and father, built up out of rice and gruel, impermanent, subject to rubbing and pressing, to dissolution and dispersion, and this is my consciousness, supported by it and bound up with it."[3] There is just far too much mental activity required to contemplate all these qualities and their interrelationships to be able to comprehend this without any thinking.

If you restrict insight practice to only being done while in the jhānas, then upon emerging from the jhānas, what should you do? Since far more of your life is going to be spent not in the jhānas, does this mean there are no insight practices to do after you leave the jhānas? Is all that time basically not useful for gaining insight?

If you feel that insight practice should be done upon emerging from the jhānas, then there are a whole host of insight practices available to engage in—see the web page "A Partial List of Insight Practices" at http://rc.leighb.com/more/A_Partial_List_of_Insight_Practices.htm. Any of these can be taken up upon emerging from the jhānas—and that includes walking meditation and eating meditation when you arise from your sitting meditation period. The huge number of possible objects of examination provides a far greater opportunity for "knowing and seeing things as they are" than does limiting your examination to the qualities of the jhānas.

In order to attain liberation, you need to become disenchanted with the things of the world that you are craving and clinging to. It's not very likely that the qualities of the jhānas are your major sources of craving and clinging. It certainly will be much more valuable to examine where you are actually caught than to take a close look at things that are not entrapping you. To do the latter is like looking for your keys where the light is good rather than where you might have lost them!

Nothing I can write in this book is going to settle this discussion. Partially that's because neither of these practices is wrong practice. Doing insight practice in a jhānic state—provided you can even do so without losing the jhāna—will indeed give you insight into the impermanent, ultimately unsatisfactoriness, and emptiness of the jhānas. No doubt that will be useful. Insight into the impermanent, ultimately unsatisfactoriness, and emptiness of the things you are craving and clinging to will also be very useful. All I can really say is that there appear to be far more places in the suttas where insight practice is taught to be done after the jhānas than in the jhānas. Furthermore the post-jhāna insight instructions seem to be part of much earlier strata of material than the in-jhāna insight instructions.

What is without a doubt is that "wisdom, when imbued with concentration, brings great fruit and profit."[4] The jhānas will certainly turbocharge your insight practice whether that practice is done in the jhānas or after the jhānas or both.

Notes

Preface

1. MN 22.38 and SN 22.86. See Bhikkhu Bodhi, "I Teach Only Suffering and the End of Suffering," *Tricycle Magazine,* Winter 2013, for a detailed discussion of this famous phrase.
2. Translation by Ven. Khantipalo.

Introduction

1. E.g., DN 22.21; MN 141.31; SN 45.8; AN 5.28.
2. MN 36.31. Bronkhorst, *Two Traditions,* section 1.5, p. 24, refers to this "passage which appears to contain very old elements (Horsch, 1964; Bareau, 1963: 47–48, 52–53)."
3. E.g., MN 8.18, 19.27, 108.15, 152.18; SN 35.146, 43.1, 43.13, 43.44, 47.10; AN 5.73–74, 7.74, 9.19.
4. E.g., DN 2–8, 10–12; MN 38.39–40, MN 64, 77; AN 5.28.
5. The faculty of concentration is defined as the four jhānas at SN 48.10. The power of concentration is defined as the four jhānas at AN 5.14.
6. E.g., DN 22.21; MN 141.31; SN 45.8; AN 5.28.
7. MN 26.15–16.

Chapter 1. The Preliminaries

1. E.g., DN 2–13; MN 27, 38, 39, 51, 53, 76, 79, 101, 107, 112, 125; AN 4.198, 5.75–76, 10.99.
2. *Ehipassiko.*
3. DN 2.64.
4. DN 22.4 and MN 10.8.

Chapter 3. Entering the Jhānas

1. DN 1.3.23.

Chapter 4. First Jhāna

1. Vsm 4.94–99, pp. 137–39.
2. Tibetan: *gtum-mo*; Sanskrit: *caṇḍālī.* The so-called mystic heat practice.

Chapter 5. Second Jhāna

1. Anguttara-Nikāya 10.72: Kaṇṭaka Sutta, "Thorns."

Chapter 7. Fourth Jhāna

1. Khema, "Who Is My Self?" 65.
2. See for example MN 18, 24, 35, 54, 66, 75, 82, 88, 97; many places in the SN as well.

Chapter 9. The Immaterial Jhānas

1. Vsm 4.100 and expanded upon in the *Abhidhammattha Saṅgaha.*

Chapter 10. With a Mind Thus Concentrated

1. Luuk Tinbergen, "The Natural Control of Insects in Pine

Woods: Factors Influencing the Intensity of Predation by Songbirds," *Archives Néerlandaises de Zoologie* 13 (1960): 265–343.

2. "Attention and the Search Image," in *Avian Visual Cognition,* edited by Robert G. Cook, Department of Psychology, Tufts University, in cooperation with Comparative Cognition Press (2001), www.pigeon.psy.tufts.edu/avc/pblough/si_attention.htm.

Chapter 11. Vitakka and Vicāra

1. See Anālayo, *Comparative Study,* 15, for more about this type of repetition.
2. Bodhi, Aṅguttara Nikāya, 1649n436.
3. Roderick S. Bucknell, "The Importance of Pali/Chinese Comparisons in Studies of Early Buddhist Doctrine," paper presented at the ninth annual conference of the Australian Association for the Study of Religions, Canberra, August 1984, p. 4.
4. See Polak, *Reexamining Jhāna,* 137–42, for a more detailed discussion of the use of the words *vitakka* and *vicāra* in the suttas.

Chapter 12. First Jhāna

1. Vsm 4.79ff. See also Pa-Auk, 2000, 102.
2. See Bucknell, "Importance of Pali/Chinese Comparisons," 4.
3. In the Chinese āgama corresponding to the Cūlavedalla Sutta (MN 44), the topic of the five factors of the first jhāna does appear—see Anālayo, *Comparative Study,* 2. The fact that it appears in a different āgama would also seem to indicate its being a late insertion.
4. *Journal of the Royal Asiatic Society,* 1902; quoted in Pande, 1995, 138.
5. Vsm 4.32, p. 122; 4.42, p. 124ff; also 4.74, p. 131ff.

Chapter 13. Second Jhāna

1. Anguttara-Nikāya 10.72: Kaṇṭaka Sutta, "Thorns."

Chapter 14. Third Jhāna

1. DN 1.3.23.
2. Anguttara-Nikāya 10.72: Kaṇṭaka Sutta, "Thorns."

Chapter 15. Fourth Jhāna

1. E.g., DN 22.11; MN 10.32; SN 36 passim.
2. See Anālayo, *Comparative Study,* 14, for more about these types of memory aids.
3. Anguttara-Nikāya 10.72: Kaṇṭaka Sutta, "Thorns."

Chapter 16. The Jhāna Summary

1. DN 2–13; MN 7, 40; SN 12.23, 35.97, 42.13, 47.10, 55.40; AN 3.95, 5.26, 6.10, 10.1–5, 11.12.
2. Bodhi, "Discourse on the Fruits," 148–52.
3. DN 2.42.

Chapter 17. Insight Knowledge

1. E.g., SN 22.59; MN 109.
2. MN 112, which is probably a late composition, uses *viññāna* in all four ways in the same sutta.

Chapter 18. The Immaterial States

1. E.g., Poṭṭhapāda Sutta (DN 9.28).
2. E.g., Mahānidāna Sutta (DN 15.2); "The City" (SN 12.65).
3. E.g., "Analysis of Dependent Origination" (SN 12.2) and many other suttas in SN 12.

4. E.g., Bronkhorst, *Two Traditions,* sections 7.2.1–4, pp. 55–67, and Polak, *Reexamining Jhāna,* 114–27.
5. Wynne, *Origin of Buddhist Meditation,* 42–62.

Chapter 19. The Cessation of Perception and Feeling

1. Vsm 12, p. 701ff. See also Pa-Auk, 2000, p. 235: "you will find that eventually all formations cease."
2. E.g., DN 9, 16; MN 25, 26, 30, 31, 43, 44, 50, 59, 111, 113.
3. Vsm 11.124, 13.18.ii.
4. See www.melafilms.com/pages/documentary.html.
5. Vsm 4.79ff. See also Pa-Auk, 2000, p. 102.
6. Roderick S. Bucknell, "Reinterpreting the Jhānas," *Journal of the International Association of Buddhist Studies* 16 (2 Winter 1993): 403 (page 403 in particular, but the whole article is very helpful for seeing this).

Chapter 20. The Psychic Powers

1. From a note to Robert S. Marcus, February 12, 1950, on the occasion of his son passing away due to polio. See http://weblog.liberatormagazine.com/2010/10/einstein-on-being-human-sayings.html.
2. E.g., MN 4.27, 19.14ff, 36.40, 85.38, 100.37.
3. See www.skeptiko.com/stuart-hameroff-on-quantum-consciousness-and-singularity/.
4. See for example the Susīma Sutta at SN 22.70 and the Khemaka Sutta at SN 22.89. Alexander Wynne discusses all three of these suttas and this split in his paper "Miraculous Transformation and Personal Identity: A Note on The First *Anātman* Teaching of the Second Sermon" (2009).

Chapter 21. Ending the Āsavas

1. Cf. AN 1.46.
2. See Pande, 1995, 86.
3. MN 36.44.
4. DN 2.97–98.

Chapter 22. Other Benefits of Jhāna Practice

1. A. Pascual-Leone, C. Freitas, L. Oberman, J. C. Horvath, M. Halko, M. Eldaief, et al., "Characterizing Brain Cortical Plasticity and Network Dynamics across the Age-Span in Health and Disease with TMS-EEG and TMS-fMRI," *Brain Topography* 24: 302–15. doi 10.1007/s10548-011-0196-8.
2. Richard J. Davidson and Antoine Lutz, "Buddha's Brain: Neuroplasticity and Meditation," *IEEE Signal Processing Magazine,* September 2007, 176.
3. Ibid., 173.
4. Massachusetts General Hospital, "Mindfulness Meditation Training Changes Brain Structure in Eight Weeks," ScienceDaily, January 21, 2011. www.sciencedaily.com/releases/2011/01/110121144007.htm.
5. Goleman, *Destructive Emotions,* ch. 8, esp. 194, and ch. 14, esp. 334–46. See also Daniel Goleman, "Finding Happiness: Cajole Your Brain to Lean to the Left," *The New York Times,* February 4, 2003, www.nytimes.com/2003/02/04/health/behavior-finding-happiness-cajole-your-brain-to-lean-to-the-left.html.
6. E.g., the phrase "the four jhānas that constitute the higher mind and are pleasant abiding here and now" occurs at MN 6.9, 53.6, 108.17, 119.36, 21.4, and over 20 times in the AN.
7. Michael R. Hagerty, Julian Isaacs, Leigh Brasington, Larry

Shupe, and Eberhard E. Fetz, "EEG Power and Coherence Analysis of an Expert Meditator in the Eight Jhānas," working paper presented at the 2008 Mind and Life Conference, available from http://leighb.com/eegjhanas.htm, p. 11.

Appendix 1. Frequently Asked Questions

1. Personal communication from Ayya Khema sometime in the period 1991–94.
2. MN 26.15–16.
3. MN 36.30.
4. MN 36.31.
5. MN 36.34.
6. Khema, *I Give You My Life,* 160.
7. MN 118.18–21; SN 54.1, 3, 4, 6–20.
8. E.g., DN 22.21; MN 141.31; SN 45.8.
9. See for example MN 18, 24, 35, 54, 66, 75, 82, 88, 97; many places in the SN as well.

Appendix 2. Helpful Things to Do at the Beginning and End of Each Meditation Period

1. Adapted from Thich Nhat Hanh, *Being Peace* (Berkeley, CA: Parallax Press, 1996), 5.
2. Dhp 113.

Appendix 3. Access Concentration Methods

1. Vsm 3.104–06, pp. 104–5.
2. E.g., DN 22.2; MN 10.4, 118.17; SN 54 (many suttas).
3. E.g., DN 22.2; MN 10.4, 118.18; SN 54 (many suttas).
4. A number of Ayya Khema's guided visualizations have been

transcribed and are available on the Internet at http://leighb.com/metta.htm.

5. DN 17.2.3–4.
6. Ajahn Amaro, "The Sound of Silence," in *Buddhadharma: The Practitioner's Quarterly,* Winter 2012.
7. Vsm 4.1–33, pp. 113–22.
8. Vsm 3–13, pp. 81–430.

Appendix 4. In or Out: The Relationship between Jhāna Practice and Insight Practice

1. Pande, 1995, "Studies in the Origin of Buddhism," 135. Anālayo, Comparative Study, 355–58 discusses the Chinese āgama corresponding to MN 64 and points out that even though insight practice is to be done while in the jhānas, the method is different.
2. E.g., DN 2.83, also found in many other suttas in the first section of DN and in MN 38.39–40, 77.26.
3. DN 2.83.
4. DN 16.1.12.

Glossary

Abhidhamma. The third division of the Pali canon, consisting of a deconstructionist, metaphysical view of the Buddha's doctrine.

adukkha and asukha. Neither painful nor pleasant, neither happiness nor unhappiness.

ajjhattaṃ sampasādana. Inner tranquility.

ānāpānasati. Mindfulness of breathing.

aṅga. Factor; a constituent part of a whole or system or collection.

arahat. A worthy one, meaning fully awakened.

āsava. Intoxicant; also translated as outflow, influx, effluent, canker, taint.

bhavataṇhā. Craving for becoming.

Bodhisatta. (Pali) The Buddha-to-be before his awakening.

bodhisattva. (Sanskrit) A being that compassionately refrains from entering nirvana in order to save others and is worshipped as a deity in Mahayana Buddhism; the personification of an archetype.

brahma-vihāra. One of four meditation practices of loving-kindness, compassion, appreciative joy, and equanimity.

cetaso. The genitive of *ceto,* which is derived from *citta,* meaning "heart/mind."

citta. Heart/mind.

citt'ekaggata. One-pointedness of mind.

dhamma. Phenomena. When capitalized, refers to the teaching of the Buddha and also "the way things truly are."

dukkha. Bummer,* unsatisfactoriness, stress, suffering.

ehipassiko. Come and see for yourself.

ekaggata. One-pointedness; see also *citt'ekaggata.*

ekodi-bhavam. Concentrated, attentive, fixed + become.

iddhi. Psychic power.

jhāna. Literally "meditation"; one of four (later eight) states of concentration.

jhāyati. To meditate.

kāmataṇhā. Sensual craving.

kāya. Group, heap, collection, body.

kāyena. Bodily, physical.

khandha. One of the five aggregates: rūpa, vedanā, saññā, sankhara, viññāṇa.

mantra. A sound, syllable, word, or group of words that is repeated silently in order to generate concentration.

mettā. Loving-kindness, unconditional love.

ñāṇa. Knowledge.

nibbāna. Literally "not burning"—that is, not buring with the fires of greed, hate, or delusion; the goal of the holy life, the realization that brings an end to *dukkha.*

nimitta. Sign. It later came to have a more specific meaning of a visual circle of light appearing as a sign of deep concentration.

pāmojja. Gladness, worldly joy.

pañña. Wisdom.

---

* See the essay "*Dukkha* is a Bummer" at http://leighb.com/bummer.htm for a detailed exploration of why "bummer" is a good translation of *dukkha.*

parinibbāna. Usually it means the death of an arahat, occasionally used synonymously with nibbāna.

passaddhakāya. Bodily tranquility.

pīti. Glee, rapture.

rūpa. Materiality, body.

saddhā. Usually translated as "faith" but perhaps more accurately as "confidence."

samatha. Calm.

samādhi. Indistractability, concentration.

sampajañña. Clear comprehension.

saṃsāra. Worldly existence, the indefinitely repeating cycles of birth, dukkha, and death.

saññā. Perception, naming, identifying, conceptualizing.

saññāvedayitanirodha. The cessation of perception and feeling.

sati. Mindfulness, remembering to be here now.

sīla. Morality, ethical behavior.

somanassa and domanassa. Joy and grief.

sukha. Happiness/joy.

sukha and dukkha. Pleasure and pain.

sutta. Discourse, teaching; the second division of the Pali canon, consisting of discourses given by the Buddha or his closest disciples.

taṇhā. Craving (literally "thirst").

upacāra-samādhi. Access concentration: fully with the object of meditation, and if there are any thoughts, they are not distracting.

upekkha. Equanimity (literally "gaze upon").

vicāra. Examining.

viññāṇa. Consciousness; occasionally it means "mind"; literally "divided knowing."

vipassanā. Insight, an understood experience.

vitakka. Thinking.

Bibliography

Primary Sources

SUTTAS

Aṅguttara Nikāya. Translated by Bhikkhu Bodhi. Somerville, MA: Wisdom Publications, 2012.

Dīgha Nikāya. Translated by Maurice Walshe. Somerville, MA: Wisdom Publications, 1995.

The Discourse on the Fruits of Recluseship. Translated by Bhikkhu Bodhi. Kandy, Sri Lanka: Buddhist Publications Society, 1989.

Majjhima Nikāya. Translated by Bhikkhu Ñāṇamoli and Bhikkhu Bodhi. Somerville, MA: Wisdom Publications, (1995).

Saṃyutta Nikāya. Translated by Bhikkhu Bodhi. Somerville, MA: Wisdom Publications, 2003.

Sutta Nipāta: The Rhinoceros Horn and Other Early Buddhist Poems. Translated by K. R. Norman. Oxford: The Pali Text Society, 1996.

The Sutta-Nipāta. Translated by Hammalawa Saddhatissa. Oxford: Routledge, 1995.

Udāna and the Itivuttaka. Translated by John D. Ireland. Kandy, Sri Lanka: Buddhist Publication Society, 1998.

The Life of the Buddha. Bhikkhu Ñanamoli. Onalaska, WA: Pariyatti Publishing, 2003.

ABHIDHAMMA

Dhammasaṅgaṇī: Buddhist Psychological Ethics. Translated by C. A. F. Rhys Davids. Oxford: Pali Text Society, 1900.

Kathāvatthu: Points of Controversy. Translated by S. Z. Aung and C. A. F. Rhys Davids. Oxford: Pali Text Society, 1915.

Puggalapaññatti: A Designation of Human Types. Translated by B. C. Law. Oxford: Pali Text Society, 1922.

Vibhaṅga: The Book of Analysis. Translated by Venerable U Thittila. Oxford: Pali Text Society, 1969.

COMMENTARIES

Paṭisambhidāmagga: The Path of Discrimination, second edition. Translated by Bhikkhu Ñāṇamoli. Oxford: The Pali Text Society, 1997.

Vimuttimagga: The Path of Freedom, by the Arahant Upatissa. Translated by Rev. N. R. M. Ehara, Soma Thera, and Kheminda Thera. Kandy, Sri Lanka: Buddhist Publication Society, 1995.

Visuddhimagga: The Path of Purification, by Bhadantacariya Buddhaghosa, fifth edition. Translated by Bhikkhu Ñāṇamoli. Kandy, Sri Lanka: Buddhist Publication Society, 1991. Available for free download from http://www.accesstoinsight.org/lib/authors/nanamoli/PathofPurification2011.pdf.

Secondary Sources

Anālayo, Ven. *A Comparative Study of the Majjhima Nikāya.* Elmhurst, NY: Dharma Drum Publishing, 2011.

Blackmore, Susan. "Near-Death Experiences: In or Out of the Body?" *Skeptical Inquirer* (Fall 1991): 16, 34–45.

Blackmore, Susan. J., and T. S. Troscianko. "The Physiology of the Tunnel." *Journal of Near-Death Studies* 8:15–28.

Brahmavamso, Ajahn Mahathera. *Mindfulness, Bliss, and Beyond: A Meditator's Handbook.* Somerville, MA: Wisdom Publications, 2006.

Bronkhorst, Johannes. *The Two Traditions of Meditation in Ancient India,* second edition. Delhi: Motilal Banarsidass, 1993 (Reprint: 2000).

Bucknell, Roderick S. "The Importance of Pali/Chinese Comparisons in Studies of Early Buddhist Doctrine," paper presented at the ninth annual conference of the Australian Association for the Study of Religions, Canberra, August 1984.

———. "Reinterpreting the Jhānas." *Journal of the International Association of Buddhist Studies* 16 (2 Winter 1993).

Buddhadasa Bhikkhu. *Mindfulness with Breathing: A Manual for Serious Beginners.* Somerville, MA: Wisdom Publications, 1996.

Catherine, Shaila. *Focused and Fearless: A Meditator's Guide to States of Deep Joy, Calm and Clarity.* Somerville, MA: Wisdom Publications, 2008.

Davids, T. W. Rhys, and W. Stede, eds. *Pali-English Dictionary.* London: PTS, 1926 (1959).

Gethin, Rupert. "On the Practice of Buddhist Meditation according to the Pali Nikāyas and Exegetical Sources." *Buddhismus in Geschichte und Gegenwart* (Hamburg) 10 (2004): 17–37.

Goleman, Daniel. *Destructive Emotions.* New York: Bantam, 2004.

Gunaratana, Mahathera Henepola. *Beyond Mindfulness in Plain*

English: An Introductory Guide to Deeper States of Meditation. Somerville, MA: Wisdom Books, 2009.

———. *The Jhānas in Theravāda Buddhist Meditation.* Kandy, Sri Lanka: Buddhist Publication Society, n.d.

Hagerty, Michael R., Julian Isaacs, Leigh Brasington, Larry Shupe, and Eberhard E. Fetz. "Case Study of Ecstatic Meditation: fMRI and EEG Evidence of Self-Stimulating a Reward System." *Neural Plasticity* 2013. http://dx.doi.org/10.1155/2013/65357 (2013).

———. "EEG Power and Coherence Analysis of an Expert Meditator in the Eight Jhānas," working paper presented at the 2008 Mind and Life Conference. Available from http://leighb.com/eegjhanas.htm.

Khema, Ayya. *Being Nobody Going Nowhere: Meditations on the Buddhist Path.* Somerville, MA: Wisdom Publications, 1988.

———. *I Give You My Life: The Autobiography of a Western Buddhist Nun.* Boston: Shambhala Publications, 1998.

———. *Visible Here and Now.* Boston: Shambhala Publications, 2001.

———. *When the Iron Eagle Flies.* New York: Arkana, 1991.

———. *Who Is My Self? A Guide to Buddhist Meditation.* Somerville, MA: Wisdom Publications, 1997.

Matara Sri Ñanarama Mahathera. *The Seven Stages of Purification and the Insight Knowledges.* Kandy, Sri Lanka: Buddhist Publication Society, 1983.

Nyanatiloka Mahathera. *Buddhist Dictionary: Manual of Buddhist Terms and Doctrines.* Kandy, Sri Lanka: Buddhist Publication Society, 1980.

Pa-Auk Sayadaw. *Knowing and Seeing: Talks and Questions-and-Answers at a Meditation Retreat in Taiwan,* second edition.

Tullera, Australia: Buddha Dharma Education Association, 2000.

Pande, Govind C. *Studies in the Origin of Buddhism.* Delhi: Motilal Banarsidass, 1995.

Polak, Grzegorz. *Reexamining Jhāna: Towards a Critical Reconstruction of Early Buddhist Soteriology.* Lublin, Poland: Wydawnictwo Uniwerystetu Marii Curie-Skłodowskiej, 2011.

Schmithausen, Lambert. "On Some Aspects of Descriptions or Theories of 'Liberating Insight' and 'Enlightenment' in Early Buddhism." In *Studien zum Jainismus und Buddhismus. Gedenkschrift für Ludwig Alsdorf,* 199–250. Wiesbaden: Franz Steiner, 1981.

Shankman, Richard. *The Experience of Samādhi: An In-depth Exploration of Buddhist Meditation.* Boston: Shambhala Publications, 2008.

Snyder, Stephen, and Tina Rasmussen. *Practicing the Jhānas: Traditional Concentration Meditation as Presented by the Venerable Pa Auk Sayadaw.* Boston: Shambhala Publications, 2009.

Sole-Leris, Amadeo. *Tranquillity and Insight.* Onalaska, WA: Pariyatti Publishing, 1992.

Stuart-Fox, Martin. "Jhāna and Buddhist Scholasticism." *Journal of the International Association of Buddhist Studies* 12 (2 Winter 1989).

Sumedho, Ajahn. *The Sound of Silence: The Selected Teachings of Ajahn Sumedho.* Somerville, MA: Wisdom Publications, 2007.

———. *The Way It Is.* Great Gaddesden, UK: Amaravati Publications, 1991.

Vajiranana, Mahathera. *Buddhist Meditation in Theory and Practice.* Kuala Lampur: Buddhist Missionary Society, 1967.

Wynne, Alexander. "Miraculous Transformation and Personal Identity: A Note on The First *Anātman* Teaching of the

Second Sermon." *Thai International Journal of Buddhist Studies* 1 (2009).

———. *The Origin of Buddhist Meditation.* Oxford: Routledge, 2007.

Acknowledgments

INTERDEPENDENT INTERRELATEDNESS means that it is impossible for me to acknowledge everyone who helped contribute to the manifestation of this book. However, I would be completely remiss if I did not acknowledge the contributions of some very key people.

The late Venerable Ayya Khema taught me to meditate, taught me the jhānas, and taught me to be a dhamma teacher. To her I owe an enormous debt of gratitude. Ajahn Buddhadasa Bhikkhu and his translator Santikaro were very helpful not only in teaching me the depths of mindfulness of breathing, but also in inspiring my early practice. Ajahn Sumedo, Ajahn Amaro, and other monastics of the Western Ajahn Chah Sangha were also instrumental in teaching me dhamma. Venerable Pa Auk Sayadaw did a masterful job of teaching the jhānas as found in the *Visuddhimagga*. Bhante U Vimalaramsi taught me the importance of relaxing between noticing a distraction and returning to the breath—a very useful addition to my practice.

Lay teachers Ruth Denison, Joseph Goldstein, Jack Kornfield, Sharon Salzberg, Kamala Masters, Gil Fronsdal, Stephen and Martine Batchelor, Kittisaro and Thanisaro, and John Peacock all have taught me much dhamma on multiple retreats. Gregory Kramer's masterful teaching of Insight Dialogue gave me insights into areas I had no idea I was missing. James Baraz's weekly sitting group in Berkeley, California, was a source of dhamma, inspiration, and friendship for more than a decade.

Translations of the suttas by Bhikkhu Bodhi, Maurice Walshe, Thanissaro Bhikkhu, John D. Ireland, and others have brought the words of the Buddha alive even today. For this my gratitude is overwhelming. They have made it possible for those of us with limited or no knowledge of Pali to access these profound teachings.

David and Kathy Forsythe, Charlene Schubert, and Brian Kelley all typed transcripts of various dhamma talks I gave on the jhānas. Without their help, I might never have felt I could even start this project. Marsha Lawson, Martha Lee Turner, John Kelly, Nandyia, and Wiley Fox read an early draft and suggested many improvements. Nancy Burnett and Anna Ossenfort provided much-needed assistance in shepherding this book to Shambhala for publication. My agent, Ted Weinstein, handled the tons of publishing details that I had no clue about, as well as initially putting me in contact with my very excellent editor, Dave O'Neal at Shambhala.

Dhammadasa and Laura Hauer of Cloud Mountain Retreat Center have been very supportive and encouraging of my teaching from the very beginning. Andy Olendzki and Mu Soeng of the Barre Center for Buddhist Studies, along with the fantastic staff there, have not only directly supported the writing of this book, but have also been a wonderful source of dhamma learning and friendship. The staff at the Insight Meditation Society, both at the Retreat Center and the Forest Refuge, have not only made my stays at IMS wonderful and easy, but have been great friends as well.

The Buddha said that "noble friends and noble conversations are the whole of the holy life." I have been enormously blessed with an abundance of noble friends with whom I've had countless noble conversations. Mary Wall urged me to attend my first retreat—for that I will always be deeply grateful to her. Gail Gokey organized the first retreat I ever taught—without that push into teaching jhānas, I would never have written this book. Nick Herzmark and I have spent countless evenings discussing the dhamma from many perspectives. Michael Freeman, Lucinda Green, Lloyd Burton, and Kevin Griffin have all shared the jhāna teaching seat with me, and I definitely benefited from our discussions during those retreats. Kevin also provided invaluable suggestions about how to structure a book in general and one about the jhānas in particular. Certainly the greatest thing about teaching meditation retreats is all the wonderful students I meet—and all that they share with me about the dhamma. The full list of my noble friends might be longer than the rest of this book, but here are some more friends who have been especially helpful, listed in the order I met them: Chuck McNeal, Eldon New, Ed White, Bill Symes, Zeida Rothman, Shaila Catherine, Amrit Khalsa, Barbara Roberts, Richard Shankman, Ron Lister, Lynn Kelly, Jill Shepherd, Judson Brewer, Luis Carvalho, Diana Clark. Minia Roth not only provided noble friendship and noble conversations, but also logistical support beyond measure—without her support, this project would have never happened.

I would be remiss if I did not mention my gratitude for the deep teachings I have received from Tsoknyi Rinpoche and H. H. the Dalai Lama. And I owe an incalculable debt of gratitude to all the millions of people who over the last two and a half millennia have preserved the Buddha's dhamma for us—and most especially to the Buddha for finding and showing the way.

May any merit from this project be to the benefit and liberation of all beings everywhere!

Index

About the Author

Leigh Brasington was born and raised in Mississippi. In 1971, he graduated from Rhodes College in Memphis with a BA in mathematics with honors, Phi Beta Kappa. He then began a more than 35-year career of "playing with computers for money." After he moved to San Francisco in 1974, he began taking extended time to travel: three years around the world in 1979–81, a year traveling in Australia and Asia in 1988, six months around the world in 1998, plus numerous shorter trips overseas as well.

He began meditating in 1985 and eventually became the senior North American student of Venerable Ayya Khema. She authorized him to teach, and he began leading residential retreats in 1997. He has taught jhānas and insight practices in over one hundred residential retreats.

Near the end of 2008, he retired from software engineering, and over the next three years, he spent 20 months in retreat at the Insight Meditation Society's Forest Refuge. It was during these half dozen long retreats that, among other investigations, he began closely examining his experiences of the jhānas and the descriptions of the jhānas found in the suttas. This book is the result of that study, coupled with many years of practicing and teaching the jhānas.